My Journey
Vol 1
John M. Suits

Copyright © 2024 by
John M. Suits

Published by:
Pine Book Writing
www.PineBookWriting.com[1]
R-10225 Yonge St Suite #250, Richmond Hill, ON L4C 3B2, Canada.

Printed in the United States of America

---

1. http://www.pinebookwriting.com/

Preface

Contained in these pages is a short collection of memories, just a few days, taken from their place in time and committed to paper. Some of these memories are somewhat dim....others as vivid as the day they happened.

All are true, and all are as accurate as memory will allow. It is not my intention to give you, the reader, a detailed account of every little thing that happened in my life, but, rather to take you on a journey that spans three-quarters of a century, and let you walk with me as parts of my life unfold. I cannot give you my life in its entirety, for some things are just better left unsaid, but hopefully, you will see some of the high and low points. Hopefully, you will experience not only the times of anguish, sadness, loneliness, and despair, but also the times of happiness, joy, love, and elation. Some of these memories are very short, maybe as little as a few sentences, others are not so short. Some of them are written in the third person, but you can be certain that the third person is me. Some of the names I have changed for obvious reasons, but otherwise, these pages tell of things as they happened. There is no embellishment. I have simply and honestly tried to paint the picture that was printed on the fabric of my mind at the time.

In these pages, you will find little snippets of my life, a little original poetry, and a few pages of things and times that were a part of the world that I lived in. These few short glimpses into my life may give the reader some idea of the experiences that made me the person that I am today.

My hope is that you will not be disappointed as you walk back to that other place and time, back to a world that was uniquely mine. My hope is that you will not only see me, the old man who writes these memories and the youth who made them, but that you will begin to see the people and things that were so much a part of my world back in the day, when life was new, scary and beautiful....and I had all the time in the world.

This, then, is a very small portion of.....

My Journey

On The Road Again

I don't remember when we moved to Eldorado from the farm in Hardin County, that was probably in 1952 or 53. We moved into a house on Second Street in Parrish addition in Eldorado Illinois. This move would be the first of eighteen in the next ten years, and I would go to no less than fourteen different schools. I don't remember too much about this house except that it had a small porch on the east side of the front, and it was on this porch that I discovered by fingerprints.

I was too young to go to school, so I was outside playing alone. I had lain down on the floor of that porch and reaching as far back under the floor boards as I could, I felt around for nothing in particular. I moved my hand this way and that when suddenly, I felt what must have been a nail point that stuck me right in the middle of the middle fingertip of my left hand. Quickly, I jerked my hand free of the porch and examined where it hurt and there, where the nail had stung my fingertip were all these rings....and believe it or not, all my other fingers had the same rings on them as well.

We moved from there, I don't know when, into a house on the corner of Fourth and Mahoney Streets. This house, I remember very well. It faced Fourth Street and had a front porch that extended all the way from one side of the house to the other. It had four columns holding up the roof of that porch and a wide set of concrete stairs that led up to the floor. There were two front doors, as was the custom of the days when the house was built. The door on the left led into the living room, the other, into the front bedroom. The side of the house that faced Mahoney Street had a porch.. It was a much smaller affair with its own set of stairs. This was the entrance into the house that was used by everyone but complete strangers.

Coming into this house from the front porch, you would step into the living room with its wallpaper sporting those large, ugly flowers. To the right was the door to my parent's bedroom; to the left, you would see a couch and easy chair, and in the corner was a small table on which the telephone sat. This phone, you didn't dial, you just picked up the receiver and the operator would say, "Number please." You would tell her what number you wanted and she would connect you.

Under the window on the east wall was my father's desk, and among other things, in that desk could be found a harmonica and a spent .50 caliber machine gun cartridge. I was always fascinated by that thing.

On the wall above the desk and beside the window hung an honest to God Cuckoo Clock. In the next corner was a couple of cypress roots as we called them, stripped of their bark, and dried and shellacked. They were used in many homes, of the time, as décor. Moving on around you would find two more chairs with a table between them and then the wide doorway into the Dining room. There was a floor furnace with its grill right in that doorway. My younger brother Gary would sometimes hand in a baby swing over that grill.

Passing through the Dining room, that sometimes doubled as a bedroom, you came into the kitchen. A small cabinet was on the right and then the back door that led to the side porch. The bathroom was on the same wall as the back door. On the south wall were the sink, stove, and cabinets. On the west wall was the refrigerator and the door to my brother, James', bedroom. My sisters, Janice and Bonnie, slept in a bedroom off the dining room. It was from this house that I started my education at Jefferson School.

When we lived in that house, we went to the Gospel Assembly Church, located only a block away on the corner of Fifth and Mahoney Streets. Church was a big part of our lives back then. We went to church on Thursday night, Saturday night, and twice on Sunday, once in the afternoon and again in the evening. My dad was pretty strict about going to church and proper behavior while we were there. He sat on the platform with other church leaders and had a bird's eye view of all his children. We had to sit on the first or second row and services would sometimes last for hours. It's easy to see how a youngster would get just a little fidgety. My dad would have none of it. If he thought we were getting a little too active or too loud and he had to give us the old, "Evil eye" or snap his fingers at us, we knew that when we got home, our butts were grass and dad was the lawnmower. We weren't allowed to give any appearance of Worldliness. No dancing, nor organized sports, we weren't allowed to sing popular songs.

Once, back then, a carnival came to town and set up on the vacant property just across Mahoney Street from our house. My dad made them put up a wrought iron fence at our property line to keep all those worldly people from overflowing into our yard. We could stand in our yard, look through the fence and watch as others ate cotton candy, played the games, and rode the rides, but we weren't allowed to take part in such things, we couldn't rub shoulders with such people. In all fairness to my dad, the fence may well have been to keep the people from trampling our grass and leaving our yard a mess of discarded paper cups and such, but that wasn't how it appeared to me.

I spent much time in the front bedroom of that house sitting beside a tape recorder, learning another church song, or some religious poem. Sometimes, it would be just scripture. The bottom line was that I didn't get to go out and play like other kids on Saturday morning. I had to learn my tape-recorded lesson first, then, and only then, when I had committed a song or poem or scripture to memory, was I allowed to go outside and play. The reason for this was that on Sunday afternoons, I would be called upon to "perform." Someone had made a small wooden box that they would put behind the Bible stand and I had to step up on that box so that I could be seen by the congregation and sing a song or quote a poem or scripture.

This was where we lived when my younger brother, Gary got his nose broken. Some of the church boys were playing baseball in our backyard when Gary, who couldn't have been more than four, just strolled right out between the catcher, an Edward Houser, the boy who was at bat. When Edward swung, at the ball, and missed, Gary was right in line and took the bat right between the eyes on the bridge of the nose. It was hospital time, instantly. There are many memories connected to that old house, some good, others, well not so much.

Sometime in early 1956, we left that house and moved to another on East Dewey Road, where a US Congressman now resides. It wasn't nearly as nice then as it is now, and we didn't stay there long. In the late winter of 1956, we were on the road again, this time to Indianapolis, Indiana. For some reason, we didn't go to church anymore, and we were free of the restraints that we had lived under to this point. We settled in at a house on a street called Home place. My uncle, Anuel Suits, already lived there, so we shared the place for a while. While we were there, I went to School #25, just a half a block away and there I finished second grade. Shortly after school let out, for the summer, we moved again, this time to a house on McCarty Street. This was move number 5 and I was seven years old. I spent the summer there on McCarty, hunting pop bottles and just being a kid.

When I could rake fifteen cents together, I'd go to the movies at the Fountain Square Theater. This was the first theater that I had ever been to in my life. This was where we lived when my Grandfather Suits passed away....my younger sister was also born when we lived here. Then, all too soon, we pulled up stakes again and moved to Morris Street, our fourth move in six months of 1956 alone. My bedroom in this house was actually a pantry for food storage. It was just large enough that a rollaway bed could be let down inside but only if the door was closed. Once the bed was let down, the door could not be opened. Now, I see how incredibly dangerous that was, but at the time, it was only another adventure.

We lived in that house through the Christmas holidays and sometime in early 1957, we were off to another place on Reno Street. I never really got the chance to get used to a house before it was time to move again, there was nothing permanent in my life, I had no school to call "My School," no permanent friends, as soon as I'd make them, I'd have to move to another place and leave them all behind. After School let out, we moved to our next house on South Illinois Ave.

On the Southwestern corner of the intersection of South Illinois and Ray Streets, there was a white concrete block building. The bottom of that building was sometimes used as a church and the top was inhabited by a black family named Flemming. We lived right next door in a double. The old black man and his wife Pearlie, loved my dad and he would spend hours sitting with the old man and drinking that "Old Crow" whiskey. This area was where white and black met. To the south was white, and north, toward the circle, was black. This was my first encounter with blacks and back in 1957, there was no love between the two races.

One night during that summer, a block or so north of us, a white man was ice-picked to death on the street. I suppose his crime was making the mistake of thinking that he could just go anywhere he wanted at any time he wanted. It didn't turn out well for him. After the deed, the blacks just melted away into the dark only to emerge thirty minutes later sporting a different Doo-rag, or different Tee-shirt. We were careful to be very close to home when night was approaching. After the summer here, it was off again to the large, grey house on the corner of Thirteenth and North Central Ave.

The neighborhood on North Central was all white. There were no racial tensions to deal with but at this place, there were no other neighborhood kids to play with either, we had to entertain ourselves.

One overcast day in the fall, I found some old rope and decided that I should put a swing on one of the lower branches of a tree standing in our back yard. In just a little while, with the help of a small board, I was happily swinging away. Swinging as high as I could, I jumped at the peak of the swing's rise and came to earth on my hands and knees. At the place where my right hand hit the ground was a piece of a broken bowl, and yep, I hit it dead center, gashing the heel of my hand so deeply that the blue muscle could be seen. Of course, I took it in to my mom, who cleaned and bandaged it up, and then she put a sling on my arm so I wouldn't be moving it around. I really needed stitches in that hand but who had money for such things as that? Anyway, I had cut myself and gone through the cleaning and bandaging of my injury without tears, or any kind of bawling, and the sling that momma put on me was my own "Red Badge of Courage."

When my dad got home, he listened to my mom's account of what happened, took a look at me and said, "Get that thing off or your arm, you ain't hurt."

And with that, he snatched it off. Just like that I went from an injured veteran of an accident with a Red Badge of Courage to show for it, to an eight-year-old stupid kid with a bloody bandage over a hand that needed stitches....and no Red Badge of Courage. It was different back then, Macho, wasn't the "In thing," it was the only thing. We saw Christmas, 1957 in this house, it would be the last Christmas that my dad would spend with us. Spring came, and with it the next move.

Three blocks further north on Central Ave, was a green double. This move, like most of the rest, meant a different school and different friends. This neighborhood had lots of kids in it, so playmates were no problem. In the other side of this double lived a man with hid dog, a Boxer, named Hercules.

I had the Measles, and my brother Joe was born while we lived in this house. In the latter part of August, a knock came to our front door, I listened as my uncle and my dad's boss told my mom that my dad was dead. I was told that my dad was in the process of buying a house for us out in Mars Hill, a housing addition in the city, but that dream died with him. The next three months, or so, were lean, hard times....and I mean, lean and hard. It was time to go, again.

The White double, in the twenty- five hundred block of North Illinois, was our next destination. This neighborhood was mixed, black and white. Every day, weather permitting, the blacks would play horse shoes in the vacant corner lot, across the street. The clanging of those steel horse shoes hitting the stakes could be heard in the neighborhood all day long. We lived here when my future sister-in-law, Phyllis, taught me how to play Chess.

After the winter of 1958-59, we moved right next door, into a house that wasn't a double, our twelfth move. I was ten years old. This was where we lived when my sister, Janice, met her future husband, Don Donnell. I went to School #56, and my mother married again to Jim Rowe, my brother Marty's dad. After the summer, we moved on to the nine hundred block of Belleview Place, out on the west side of the city.

Belleview was an all-white neighborhood at the time and actually a pretty good place to live. It was a white house with an upstairs. We were there for the fall and winter of 1959-1960 and then on the road again to Leonard Street, over in the Fountain Square area.

The house on Leonard Street was another double with an upstairs. It was a brick house and had a garage behind it that was accessible from the alley. Another school, new friends, and thankfully, this would be the last place that we would live in Indianapolis. Jim Rowe left us while we lived in this house. I don't know all the circumstances surrounding his leaving, but my mother was pregnant at the time. I never saw him again. School was out, Cherries were ripening on the neighbor's tree and summer was here. The woman who lived in the other side of this house was named Birdie. My mother made an agreement with her to store our furniture in her half of the garage while we went to New Mexico for the summer, and just like that, we were off to the Land of Enchantment. My brother, James, joined the United States Marine Corps when we left this house. After three months of staying with my sister Janice and her husband Don, in New Mexico, we boarded a train and made the trip back to Indianapolis. We went back to Leonard Street to get our furniture and guess what....? Birdie didn't want to give it up. Fact was, she had already moved some of our stuff into her house and was claiming it as her own. My mother got the police involved and we got our furniture back. Somehow, Birdie's cousin, Buddy was employed to haul our furniture back to Illinois, and soon, trailer in tow, we were on the road again. Now Buddy was a drinking man and wasted no time digging into his stash, and by the time we got to Carmi, he was pretty well lit up. We stopped for gas and while we were there, my mom called the Police. We got away from Carmi before the police got there but they caught up just outside of town. They pulled us over and questioned Buddy about how many he'd had, he said one and my mom was leaning out the car window, flashing all her fingers and thumbs at the cops. They took Buddy to jail, but that left us stranded on the side of the road. The police took mom back to Carmi and a telephone, where she called a couple of her uncles, Ed and Dick Lane. They came up to Carmi from Cave-in-Rock, loaded all our stuff on their trailer and took us to Hardin County. While momma tried to get us a place to live in Eldorado, my brother Gary and I were shipped off to Uncle Paris and Aunt Francis Pennell's house, while our sister Bonnie, and youngest brother, Joe stayed with momma at one of our aunt's house. When school started, I went to Shoemaker School with my cousins, Betty Bonnie, Shirley Gail, and Gene. October came and with it another move.

We would be going back to Eldorado, back where we were four and a half years earlier. The unit in the Eldorado Housing Project, 4B, was small but efficient, living room, kitchen, and pantry downstairs and three bedroom and bathroom up. At least we were all together again. I went to the sixth grade at Jefferson school. In November of that year, my youngest brother, Marty, was born. During our stay there of just under a year, somehow, momma purchased a house at 1209 First Street from Miss Iva Gross and we moved in, in the summer of 1961. Finally, my mother had given us a home that we weren't going to move from....and with it, a sense of permanence, of belonging, in my life. I lived in this house until 1969, when I joined the United States Army. I lived in this house longer than any other place from the time I was born until I left for the military.

Sadly, at this writing, of all the places that I have lived, from my birth to the age of twenty, all except three are gone, the house on Dewey Road, Belleview in Indianapolis, and the housing project in Eldorado. All the rest have fallen victim to time and progress. Of all those places, the only things that remain are memories.

The Drugstore

I lived on South Illinois Avenue at the time. It was a place where the White neighborhood met the Black. It wasn't the first time that I'd came into contact with blacks., I'd gone to school with a few of them at School #25 and #38, but that was school. Here, I lived right next to them.

Our house, what we called a double back in the day, was the second building south of the intersection of Ray St. and S. Illinois Ave, and was on the west side of Illinois Ave. The white building next to us, on the corner, was a two-story affair, and there was no grass between the two buildings only concrete. The bottom of this structure served as a church, sometimes, while the top was inhabited by a family named Flemming.

It was the summer of 1957. As the rising sun lit up our little portion of the world, I was already up, dressed, and on the hunt. The quarry today was those coveted pieces of glass called pop bottles. These things could be taken to any grocery store and sold for two cents each, a small fortune in the eyes of a kid, the big prize, though was the large Canada Dry Ginger Ale bottle. If you found one of these, you had found the motherlode. These large pieces of green glass fold for a whole nickel.

Dexter, my little black friend, and I took turns pulling his rusty little wagon up and down the concrete alleyways of our neighborhood and beyond. The squeaking of the wheels that announced our arrival fell on the deaf ears of sleeping residents. Somewhere, a dog barked as the sleeping city began to groan itself back to life. As we checked people's trash, with little success, it was beginning to look as though this was going to be another dry run. Turning into an alley, several blocks from our neighborhood, I ran across a discarded toy cash register, into the wagon it went. Further down the alley, pulling back the flap of a trash filled cardboard box, I discovered the motherlode! There it was, that large green bottle that represented ten pieces of bubble gum, five pieces of penny candy or a whole Snickers candy bar. We were elated. We were ecstatic. We quickly decided to call off the hunt and get to the nearest grocery store. Our hunt this morning had netted us exactly nine cents, that meant one candy bar and eight pieces of bubble gum. We were set for the day.

Arriving back home, happily chewing a mouthful of Bazooka Bubble Gum, we turned our attention to our newfound cash register. It was just a beat-up old toy that some other luckier kid had used till it was worn out. The red paint was all but gone, and the keys didn't work well anymore. Still, it was more than we had so we happily set about playing and trying to get the drawer to open. After a little while, and much knocking, banging, and prying, the drawer finally, and grudgingly, opened, and there, folded into a small, greenish rectangle, unbelievably, lay a One Dollar Bill.

This find was just more than we could ever have dreamed of. Just imagine, A WHOLE DOLLAR! Fifty cents each. This was more money than either one of us had ever had at one time. We were in heaven. In jubilation we laid our plans to dispose of this windfall. There was, of course, more candy bars and bubble gum to be bought, but this time, there was money enough for the king of all treats; Ice Cream. That blue and white Mr. Softie truck would be coming down our street about 7:00 in the evening, and I would be there, money in hand....in the meantime, though, there was always the drugstore.

Down on the corner of Morris and Meridian streets, a few blocks south and east of us, there was a drugstore. Coming through the large glass door, off of Morris Street, about ten feet to your front, you would see a long bar, black on top with those little stainless steel napkin holders placed about every four or five feet. Behind the bar was an array of glasses, dishes, spoons, and straws designed to hold and enjoy ice cream or soda or both, and the soda machine and cooler that held every flavor of ice cream known to man, or so it seemed to me. On the customer side of the bar were those red, swiveling stools sitting atop shiny metal pedestals that were fixed to the floor. Looking to the left you would see four red booths sitting against the outside wall and the actual pharmacy at the far end of the room. All this sat upon a floor of black and white tile that had been installed in a checkered pattern.

Pulling my skinny frame up onto one of those red stools, I ordered a two-scoop, strawberry ice cream cone. There were two other people in the room besides the young lady who worked the soda fountain. A sandyhaired man, wearing faded blue jeans and a white T-shirt and looking to be bout thirty, sat in the first booth and to my left, about four stools down, sat an old man, who looked to be sixty fire or seventy years old. Time had wrinkled his face and gnarled his hands. His hair was white and shaggy and needed cutting. Behind the growth of white stubble that covered that wrinkled face and neck was a toothless smile. A rather square nose, whose tip, with all the broken blood vessels, resembled a road map, jutted out separating the narrow, deep set, faded blue eyes that rested under eyebrows, who's long, unruly hairs should have been trimmed long ago.

My ice cream came, and as I sat happily enjoying my little fist full of heaven, for reasons now lost to my memory, an argument broke out between these two men. Voices rose in pitch, becoming sharp yells and tempers flared. The younger man then suddenly lunged up from his seat in the booth and hit the old man right in that square, roadmap of a nose, knocking him completely off his barstool and onto the floor behind me. I watched in amazement as the old man lay there on his back. His eyes were glassy, a mixture of blood and snot was oozing, dripping from his obviously broken nose and staining the stubble on his face and the collar and front of his blue denim shirt. He kept reaching up as though he were trying to reach something that only he could see. In those faded blue eyes and on that face, was fear, surprise, confusion, defeat...... it was as though he was trying to understand what had just occurred, but didn't have the mental tools to grasp it. In my young heart, I pitied him. It was my first encounter with adult violence. I was amazed.

It was a long time ago,

It was only a moment ago

I was eight years old...........

The Day the World Stood Still

It was late summer, 1958, another sunny summer day. The hot, humid morning air was more than muggy. It was oppressive; heavy with the promise of afternoon misery and the smells of the city. The city noise had started early, and the blaring of car and truck horns, traffic, and people could be heard clearly throughout the neighborhood. There were no clouds in the azure blue sky, and it promised to be another blissful day of play in the neighborhood. I didn't have a care in the world......all that would change today.... at least for the foreseeable future.

We had come to Indianapolis, two years earlier, in the late spring of 1956. We had an uncle there, my father's brother, who would help my dad get badly needed work. At this time, we lived in a light green duplex house in the 1500 block of North Central Avenue. Central, was a four-lane street back then and there was plenty of traffic. In front of our house, there was a short retaining wall next to the sidewalk and four or five concrete stairs brought you up to the small front yard...if it could be called a yard. Five more stairs put you on our front porch. Entering the front door, you would step into a small foyer, about five feet wide and eight feet long. Once inside, you would turn to your left to enter a small living room and then, back to your right to enter the dining room, kitchen, bathroom, etc. There was a stairway in the dining room that led to the second floor. This is where all the bedrooms were located. The walls in this house were all covered with wallpaper, the kind with all those large, gaudy flowers, I never did care for those. It seemed to me that this house was always dark.

My sisters, Bonnie and Janice, and I, would play Rummy or Old Maid in the evenings, in the dining room, while momma puttered around in the kitchen. My younger brother, Gary, kept his eyes on the small Crosley TV screen as Johnny Mac Brown rounded up the gang of outlaws, and my baby brother, Joe, born only a month or so age, made it his business to holler and squall at the top of his lungs till someone came and stuffed a bottle in his mouth or changed his diaper. James, my oldest brother, was always gone, but then, he was 16 and had a car. There were six of us kids back then, ranging in age from two months to 16 years. Life, for a kid, was pretty simple. The summer days were filled with play, bottle hunting, or some other enterprise that would usually result in someone getting their hind parts tanned with a switch.

Sometime in the mid-morning, a firm and insistent knock came on our front door. Standing beside my mother as she opened the door, I looked into the somber faces of my uncle, Anuel Suits, and my dad's boss, Marty. There was no greeting, no chit chat, for these men realized that there were no words that would soften the impact of what they had to say. Three words that would change our lives forever, "Weldon is dead!"

Instantly, overcome with grief and despair, I ran out the door and down the steps. I sat on the retainer wall, and cried. I was afraid, confused, for in my young mind, I couldn't conceive of life without my dad in it. I didn't really understand death, yet I was old enough to understand the finality of it and I knew that my dad wouldn't be coming home anymore. At this moment, I needed reassurance, I needed answers, I needed someone's arms around me, and a soothing voice telling me that everything would be just fine, but at this moment, there were none of these, so, in the utter despair of this moment, I fought that despair with the only weapon I had at my disposal, tears. My world had come crashing down, my dad was gone, forever. It had been a heart attack...he was thirty-five years old.

I had no way of knowing back then, but with those words, the weight of the world must have come crashing down on my mother's shoulders. Not only had she lost her husband, her partner, but, "Weldon is dead" meant that she would have to continue life's struggle unaided, alone. Instantly, she had been left with six children to care for. "Weldon id dead" meant that in addition to being the mother, she must now be the father also, the provider, the strength of our family, a role that she wasn't prepared for, but one that she accepted and excelled at. What would she do? What COULD she do? At that time, there were very few, if any programs to help the poor...simply put, if you didn't work, you didn't eat.

It was 1958, the same year that the Soviet Union launched Sputnik 3. The wheels of government didn't turn any faster then than they do now, and it took about three months for my mother to start receiving my dad's Social Security....and those were lean times. We ate a lot of oatmeal, homemade biscuits, and meal gravy, and almost anything else that we could get our hands on. Janice, my older sister, and I, would go after dark, to the trash bin behind the Standard Grocery store up the street from our house, and go through the produce that they had thrown away that evening. Sometimes, we'd get lucky and find a head of lettuce or some other vegetables...you could cut out the rotten part, and the rest was supper. We ate more than a few salads made from throwaways from that trash bin. Hard times require hard things.

My future sister-in-law's mother, Uneda Burgess, worked at the RCA factory in Indianapolis. At that time, RCA had a program that would help the poor with at least some winter clothing...the trick was that an employee had to recommend you.

Well, Uneda DID recommend us and before the winter snows flew, we all had new coats, gloves, shoes, socks, etc. My new coat was red, with those long wooden buttons that slipped through loops to hold the front closed, and Lordy....it had a hood. I'd never had a coat with a hood. I was proud, to say the least. The shoes were the same kind that my mom and dad always bought for my brother Gary and me., Clod hoppers, those black, leather, ankle high shoes that a lot of country boys wore back then. (This was before people threw their old shoes away. Instead, they were taken to the shoe shop and repaired, if you had the money, with new heels, new soles, heel taps, etc.) They were cheap, lasted a long time and right about now, I loved them. If you've ever had put cardboard in your shoes to cover the holes in the soles and try to keep the snow out of your socks, you'll have some idea of why I was happy to wear those new Clod Hoppers. If you've never had to do this, then you've missed a great motivational experience. Uneda Burgess, from Kentucky, was a good woman, and she was loved by many besides those in her immediate family.

I can only guess at what twists and turns my life might have taken had the events of August 28th, 1958, not happened. There is one thing that is certain, however, and that is that my life changed forever back on that warm August day in 1958, the day the world stood still.........I was nine years old.

The Land of Enchantment

We were on our way. Packed like sardines inside that '57 Chevy, nine of us were fidgeting and squirming, trying to get comfortable in a space that was made for six. The trunk was full, too. It contained our clothes, the spare tire and jack in case we had a flat; tools in case we had a mechanical problem and last, but certainly not least, the all-important cooler.

The cooler that we had was one of those light green, stamped metal affairs with a lid that was detached. It was old already, and had seen better days, but in spite of the rust on the outside, the inside was still use-worthy and kept the bologna and cheese cool enough to be edible for a while. There were no Cokes of Pepsis in that cooler, or any other kind of sodas or snacks, only the bare necessities. There was no room for extras and no money for frills, the cooler contained bologna, cheese, and ice. These items would be our meals for the next two days. Our water was a whole different thing. It was kept in what we called a "Water Bag" back then. This was a heavy, tightly woven canvas bag that would be hung on the front of the car, and the water inside would be used for drinking, and/ or adding to the radiator water level. See, back then, we didn't have plastic jugs that could be refilled with water and hauled around everywhere you went. The containers of the day were glass bottles and wax-coated paper cartons.

Our little crew of nine consisted of my mother, my two older sisters, Janice and Bonnie, my two younger brothers, Gary and Joe, my niece, Johnna, Janice's husband, Don Donnell, his friend and owner of the car, Laverne, and me.

We were in the country now. The air was different, the sounds were different and in spite of the cramped conditions, we were all happy to be on the road. We had left the city of Indianapolis early. And with it, we left the noise, smells, sights, and sounds that we had become so accustomed to. The tall, grey concrete buildings and the rows upon rows of tightly packed houses had faded far behind us as we started this new adventure. We were going to New Mexico, the desert southwest, the land of the cowboy and the Navajo Indians, it promised to be an interesting summer.

It seemed as if it would take forever to get to this wonderland, this place they called New Mexico. I had only seen it in movies, where, on Saturday mornings, Johnny Mac Brown, Tex Ritter, Rocky Lane or some other cowboy hero of mine would ride through that western wonderland cleaning up the outlaws, saving the herd, or bringing back the bank's money. We had only just started, and I was already tired of riding. I wanted to be there now. Such is the patience of a youngster when a dream is coming true before his eyes. Sometimes, if you're not careful, the anticipation of the arrival will cause you to miss the beauty of the journey. There were thirteen hundred miles of highway and with all the food, nature, fuel, and leg-stretching stops, about a day and a half of constant travel between our destination and us, but in my mind, I was already there.

Leaving the prairie country of central Illinois, we crossed the big river and got on Route 66 at Saint Louis, Missouri. Traveling southwest through the heart of the "Show Me" state and looking out through the window of the moving car, we watched as the ground rose up to make the peaks of the Ozark Mountains and ten, fell away on the other side to make a deep valley with a glistening, running stream at the bottom....and then, rise again to another peak. The hardwood trees were clothed in their finest summer apparel and appeared in every shade of green imaginable. This place was stunning in its beauty, and we were sorry to see it disappear behind us.

Darkness fell, and somewhere along the way, Don and Lavern changed places behind the steering wheel and our little sardine can continued on through the night, stopping only when Nature, or the fuel tank called. When the sun came up in the morning, we stopped at a lonely old filling station somewhere on the far western side of the Texas pan handle. The fuel tank and nature had called. We stretched our legs and refilled the water bag as we waited for Momma to dole out those bologna and cheese sandwiches. We had been seeing signs for a few miles that read, "See the Snake Pit!" These signs had pictures of big, ferocious-looking rattlesnakes painted on them that were obviously there to gouge the imagination of travelers like us and make us want to stop and take a look....and buy candy bars, chips, and gasoline. We stopped to take a look alright, and bought gasoline, but that was all. The snake pit was nothing spectacular, just a hole in the ground, about eight feet deep with a stone well curb on top. The well curb was covered with a heavy metal screen to keep the terminally stupid from trying to touch the snakes, who only numbered about four or five. The snakes, although few in number, put on a first-rate show for us as they began to rattle their tails and slither into the S-coil at our appearance at the top. It was free, it was entertaining and it was something like us kids had never seen....to us, it was worth the stop.

Mid-morning found us rolling into Grants, New Mexico, a small town that lay midways between Albuquerque and the Arizona border, we were finally here in the land of enchantment. I had two uncles, (my father's brothers) who lived here with their families and worked in the uranium mines. It was a joyous reunion for me. My cousins, Bobby, Larry, Leon, Brenda, and Jeannie were there waiting for us. I hadn't seen them since my dad's funeral, almost two years earlier. Bobby and Larry were already in their late teens, but Leon, although slightly older, was still closer to my age. They lived in a trailer court in a section of Grants called Milan Station.

Peering from under the brim of my brother in laws white, flat crowned cowboy hat, I took in what would be my home for the summer. This desert country was so different from anything that I had ever actually seen. Red rock and sand was everywhere. Off in the distance could be seen the blue outlines of a distant mountain range. Turning to the northeast, my eyes fell upon the thing that would keep me occupied for the biggest part of the summer. Black Mesa.

Black Mesa stood imposing and alone in the desert across Rt. 66 and northeast of Milan Station. This great flat-topped mountain of earth and stone rose hundreds of feet above the desert floor. Its base was totally surrounded by a gigantic jumble of boulders that had fallen away from the mountain in some cataclysm of long ago. The rock formations were mostly of lava rock or basalt, with some sandstone thrown in. It was the perfect place for an eleven-year-old cowboy wannabe to spend the summer exploring. The desert floor, between me and that mesa, was fraught with danger. Besides all the obvious dangers of the local plant life, The Cholla Cactus, and the great expanses of Prickly Pear, there were also the ever-present dangers of the western rattlesnakes, beaded lizards, and the scorpions. I would have to cross about a mile of that desert to get to the jumble of boulders and the mesa beyond, but cross it I would, first though, I would have to try to convince my cousin Leon to guide me.

Leon, as it turned out, needed no convincing. He had been to that mesa many times and never tired of going to see it just one more time. He was born an explorer, always looking just a little further over the next hilltop or pushing just a little further around the next bend in the creek. What better guide could I have had than Leon, one who was well acquainted with the place and the dangers that it presented? I trusted him completely and was more than willing to follow where he led.

The very next morning, before the sun could peek over the rim of the mesa and shed its warming light over the sleepy little town of Milan, Leon and I had already crossed Rt. 66 and the railroad tracks and were halfway to the mesa.

"How many times have you been up here?" I asked Leon, from under my borrowed white, flat-crowned cowboy hat.

"I lost count a long time ago." He answered without a thought, "Seems like a thousand."

"What's up there?" I asked, wanting to know everything at once. "What'll we do when we get there?"

"Well," he said, philosophically, as if the three years difference in our ages had allowed him to have a much deeper understanding of the mysteries of the universe, "I'll do what I always do up here, but you, you're gonna start learning about the desert. Do you remember, back home, we had those little grey lizards with the blue stripes running down their sides that we called Scorpions?"

"Yeah," I answered, remembering the bright, almost iridescent colors. "They're everywhere back home."

"Well," he said again, "They're not really Scorpions, they're really just lizards. Out here, they have real scorpions. They look like a big, pale tan spider with a long tail that curves up over its back. They don't bite ya, they've got a stinger on the tip of their tails and they sting. They're poison and they can kill ya."

Thus, my education about the desert began. I wouldn't be there long enough to become as proficient as Leon, but what little I learned did serve me well...at least on one occasion. On one of our excursions to the mesa, a tiny movement on the ground in front of me and to my left caught my eye. (Leon was always telling me to "Watch the ground in front of you, watch where you step.") I stopped, quickly, and there on the ground, trying to get under a desert, bush was a big, pale tan spider with a long tail stretched out behind it, I had stumbled upon a real scorpion. Instantly, Leon's admonition sprang to my mind. This thing wasn't something that you played with, this thing, could be death staring you in the face. Still, I had to get a closer look so I broke a branch from a nearby bush and prodded this creature until it turned to face me with its tail and stinger curled up over its back and at the ready. Seeing that it didn't want to play anymore and was actually getting ready to fight, I finally heeded Leon's warning and left the thing alone, probably the wisest thing I could possibly have done at the time. This was my one and only encounter with Scorpions, snakes, or any other dangerous desert dweller in The Land of Enchantment. It was OK, though, because the rock field at the base of the mesa, which contained boulders, some of which were larger than houses, kept us busy exploring for hours upon hours. Many times, we would just sit, perched atop one of those huge boulders, and from a mile away and a couple of hundred feet higher, we would count the cars in the train rolling down the tracks beside Rt. 66.

Time passed quickly, and before I knew it, it was August. My time in the Navajo country was slipping away. Still, I would be here till the latter part of the month, and that was far away, or so I thought. A car that I had never seen before rolled to a stop at Uncle Arlen's trailer. Much to my surprise, the doors opened and out stepped my cousins, Virgil and Frances, my uncle Joe Suits and his wife, my aunt Callie, my aunt Amy Gosser, (my dad's sister) and my grandmother, Gradie Suits. I was overjoyed to see them. This was the biggest reunion with my family that I had been to in a long time. Their stay was much too brief, but we crammed a lot of living into our time with them. We had cookouts and even a picnic on the slopes of Mt. Taylor. The best times, though, were those spent with Leon and Virgil on the mesa.

August was coming to a close. It was time for us to leave New Mexico and head back east. Five of us boarded the train and settled in for the thirteen-hundred-mile return trip back to Indianapolis. As we boarded the train and found our seats, through the windows, we waved our tearful goodbyes to cousins, uncles, and aunts. The train began to roll, slowly at first, picking up speed as it went. I could hear the audible "Clack" as the wheels of the train passed over each joint in the tracks. I wondered, as we traveled faster and faster on the rails, was this to be a new adventure? What awaited us when we got back to the city? What would we see on the way? I settled back in the uncomfortable seat and closed my eyes. Whatever awaited us would still be there after a bologna sandwich and a nap.

The year was 1960, the year that my older brother, James, joined the United States Marine Corps. Eight years later, I would follow him and join the United States Army.

.I was eleven years old, it was only the blink of an eye ago..........

Grasshoppers

Virgil, my cousin, was the quintessential country boy. He lived on the Karber's Ridge gravel, in Hardin County, Illinois with his dad, my uncle Joe, in a wood frame house located on a hill top about five miles from Rt. 1. The house sat back off of the gravel about a hundred feet or so, and faced the north. It had four Cedar posts, supporting the front porch that were about six inches in diameter and had been painted white. There was a Castor Bean growing at the east end of that porch and chains supported a porch swing on the other end. Many early mornings were spent there, in that swing taking in the morning haze, the offerings of the song birds or the sound of the rain on the tin roof as it gave its life renewing moisture to the hill top. Like many country houses at the time, Virgil's house had two front doors. The door on the east side opened into the living room, the west door, into Uncle Joe's bedroom. Like so many houses of the time, the floor was one layer of wide, rough-cut oak planks laid diagonally across the floor joists. These planks would be sanded just enough to knock off the rough and then would be covered with a few layers of old newspaper or, if one could afford it, Tar-paper. The floor was then covered with cheap linoleum. This would stop the breeze from coming through the floor in the winter and the mosquitoes in the summer. This house had two walls. One from front to back and one from side to side. These walls divided the house into four equal rooms: two bedrooms, the living room, and the kitchen. Entering the living room, you would see the Warm Morning coal stove with the coffee table and couch beyond. To the left, you would find an easy chair and the television with a scattering of potted plants. As you walked into the kitchen, you would see the back door to your front, and to the left, you would find a small refrigerator, cook stove, and sink. White enameled cabinets hung on the wall over these kitchen fixtures. The table and chairs sat between the back door and the entrance to Virgil's room. Inside the kitchen, also, was the stairway to what we called the basement. Actually, it was a root cellar with shelves to hold home canned food, potatoes, onions, whatever could be grown in the garden and kept through the winter. Uncle Joe had also installed a water pump, pressure tank, and drain in that cellar so that showers could be taken there with a garden hose. Lifebuoy, was the soap of the day. The door behind the table led to Virgil's room with its bed in the southwest outside corner and its .22 rifle and .12-gauge shotgun hanging on his home-made gun rack. The closed in back porch, off of the kitchen, would later be an entrance to another small bedroom that would be added to the house. The whole affair was covered with dark green, or brown siding that was supposed to look like brick, and it was topped off with a corrugated tin roof. Virgil's home place came complete with an outhouse, a small shed that, at one time, housed Bessie, the mild cow, and a Peachtree that grew beside the well-used garden spot.

It was a Saturday morning in 1961, and I was spending the weekend with Virgil. I hadn't slept much during the night, for the anticipation of today's fishing trip just wouldn't let my eyes close for more than an hour at a time. Rising just before the sun and silently slipping into faded blue jeans, white T-shirts, and tennis shoes, in the half-light of the coming dawn, we stepped out on the front porch and took our places in the beloved porch swing. The rhythmic creaking of the chains could be heard as we began munching on the bologna sandwiches that we had made for breakfast, we began, making our plans.

"You got any fishin' poles?" I asked, not knowing that Virgil, having done this many times before, had already thought this through.

"We'll cut us a pole or two when we get there." He said, "That way, we won't have to carry our poles all the way down there to the creek. We'll just put some line, hooks an' bobbers in our pockets an' go." Virgil always had a pocket knife. "What'll we use for bait?" I asked.

"Grasshoppers." He said matter-of-factly. "We'll take us a jar with some holes in the lid and catch us some grasshoppers on the way."

By now, the sun was on the rise and we stepped out into that fading morning mist. At the end of the dirt driveway, we turned west out on the gravel and headed towards Mug Lampert's place, a mile or so on down the road. Walking in the tire tracks of the road because that was the smoothest place, we raised little puffs of dust with every step. Ol' Lupe, Virgil's big, mostly black, German Shepard dog, led the way head low, always watching. Walking down that gravel road with Ol' Lupe, early in the morning, we were quite a picture. Looking ahead, as we started to descend the hill, I could see that the road was as straight as a string for about three-quarters of a mile and then curved to the right. There were Pine trees growing on both sides of the road most of the way. Virgil said that they had been planted there by the government, some years before. Reaching the curve, we turned off the gravel, back to our left, climbed over the locked gate, and after walking about a hundred feet, we were standing in a meadow in waist high grass, grasshoppers were everywhere. Using the jar with the holes in the lid, we caught enough grasshoppers to fish for a week. (if the truth was known, we had so many because we had as much fun catching grasshoppers as we did fishing.) After catching our bait, we walked on through the meadow and stepped into the hardwood forest. There was a small creek about thirty yards into that forest. It was about twenty feet across, contained a jumble of sandstone rocks, and was confined by steep banks. The water in this fishin' hole was five or six feet deep, dark, sea green and, as I would soon discover, was full of pan-sized Bluegill. It was a shaded spot where the sun only filtered through the trees in tiny patches here and there. The forest floor was covered with a thick blanket of last year's leaves, and they made a crunching sound with each step we took. It was secluded, it was quiet....it was heaven.

"This is it." Virgil said, taking a Barlow, bone-handled pocket knife from the pocket of his jeans, and with the skill of someone practiced in this particular art, he cut a couple of saplings of sufficient thickness and length to make fishing poles, trimmed the leaves and branches and tied on about ten feet of fishing line. Next, he pulled a small packet of hooks from his pocket, selected just the right one, and tied it on the end of the line.

"Bluegills got a little mouth," he said, "You gotta use a little hook." Taking a split shot and a small cork bobber from his pocket, he attached them to his fishing line, the split shot about six inches from the hook, and the cork, about thirty inches further up. Next, he took one of those grasshoppers from the jar, threaded it on the hook through the abdomen, and dropped it into that dark, sea-green water. Almost instantly, the cork disappeared beneath the surface with a violence that made droplets of water jump up into the air, and just as instantly, the silence was shattered by whoops and yells. "I've got one, I've got one!"

Fashioning a stringer from a small stick and more fishing line, in no time, we had his fish, the start of our supper, securely strung and tied to a tree root that was growing out of the creek bank. I couldn't get my rig put together, and in the water, fast enough. Soon, the woods around us, was alive with a chorus of the whoops and hollers of excited youth. The woods were bursting with the joyful noise of exuberance and boyhood. In that long ago time, we were happy.

After a couple of hours of fishing and catching what we thought would be enough fish to make a heaping platter for supper, we decided to go for a swim. Laying our poles and bait jar aside, we shucked our clothes and bailed off into the fishing hole, instantly discovering that not only was that dark, sea-green water deep, it was also right chilly. Shrieking with delight and the joy of the moment, we happily swam and splashed and bobbed up and down in the water. Pretending to be sharks, whales, and deep-sea divers. We spit water, splashed each other, and frolicked until we were worn out. Climbing out of the creek, we dried off as best we could with our T-shirts and got dressed again.

From somewhere, seemingly far away, we heard the sound of a car horn. Beeeeep, Beeeeep, beep, beep beep.

"We gotta go," Virgil said, "That's dad, wanting us to come."

"How do you know?" I asked, puzzled that Virgil could know who was honking the horn.

Patiently, Virgil answered. "That's the Suits call, two longs and three shorts. It's a signal that all the Suits' used years ago when they lived on the old farm...my dad, your dad, and all of our uncles would use it when they needed help with something. They'd just blow that two longs and three shorts, and everybody on the farm would know that someone in the family needed help with something." (I verified this later in life...it wasn't exactly as Virgil thought, but, in essence, it was true.)

Leaving our fish strung to the tree root, we hurried out to the road to find Uncle Joe waiting patiently for us to appear. He had come to see if Virgil and I would like to take a short trip to High Knob Tower. Enthusiastically, we agreed and since our fish were still in the cold water, we knew that they would be just fine when we returned from our trip. Later, after we had spent a couple of hours at High Knob, climbing up and down the tower and taking in the magnificence that the Southern Illinois forest is, Uncle Joe dropped us off at the locked gate and waited for us to retrieve our fish. Running through the field of waist-high grass and all the grasshoppers in the world, we once again came to the creek. This time, though, something was different. As I reached down to pull up our fish, a long, striped critter came up also. In our absence, the forest and creek had resumed its former silence and serenity, and our no shouldered friend had discovered a free meal, all strung up and unable to get away. After swallowing the first fish, the snake had discovered that now, it too, was trapped on the stringer. Carefully cutting the line that was our stringer, Virgil freed the snake, with its lunch, and salvaged the rest of our catch.

Sitting at the oil cloth covered table, later that evening, happily munching on the catch of the day, and proud that we had furnished the main course, we excitedly told and retold the adventures of the day. We were happy....and rightfully so. We were young and full of life, and, this day had been full of special adventures. This day had been one of many that Virgil and I would share before that day in April twenty years later.

Sadly, they are all gone, the house, the people, even the fishing hole. Now, only head stones, memories such as mine, and a few photos are left. There is no trace of the house where Virgil grew up. It's as if it never existed. The creek that once supported the fishing hole that brought us so much joy when we were young, is now only a dried-up bed with just a trickle of water. Time marches on, and nothing remains the same for long.

I was twelve years old back then....

Diskobolos

From the time I was old enough to read, I've been a fan of history especially ancient history. I would pick up book after book about the ancient Phoenicians, Romans, Goths, Vikings, and Greeks. Anything that was about other cultures, especially Middle Eastern or European, would keep me entertained for hours. At an early age I was reading about Roman and Greek Mythology. As I read Homer's Iliad, the story of the Trojan War, I thrilled to the exploits of Achilles and his Myrmidons, of the great Diomedes, of Ajax the Greater, and Ajax the Lesser, Agamemnon the Greek King and Odysseus, King of Ithaca. The Trojans had their heroes in Hector, Sarpedon, Aeneas and others, and even the Gods had their favorites on both sides. I read of the ancient Olympics and saw photographs of The Diskobolos, or the Discus Thrower, by the ancient sculptor Myron....and I was hooked. "Someday," I thought, looking at the photo of Myron's sculpture, "Somewhere, I'll get my hands on one of those things and when I do, I'll throw it a mile!"

In the spring of 1961, my 6th grade teacher, Mr. Jerry Johnson, posted a notice on our bulletin board that said that there was going to be a track meet at Hillcrest school for all the 5th and 6th grade boys who cared to participate. I didn't really know what a track meet was so I asked Mr. Johnson.

"Well," says he, "A track meet is where a bunch of guys get together and have races of 100 yards, 200 yards, half a mile...different distances, and field events like the shot put, and discus throw and jumping contests......"

"Wait," I said, interrupting him mid-sentence, "Discus? Did you say discus?"

"Yes," he said, "It's a round thing that they throw for distance."

I didn't even hear the last part, "Where do I sign up?" I said in elation. All I could think about was that I would finally get to toss that discus. The truth was that I had never even seen a real one. I didn't have the foggiest notion of how to even start to throw one... I only knew that I was going to be among a group of guys that were going to throw the discus, just like the ancient Greeks that I had read about I was going to do just great.

My school, Jefferson, had no discus, and no one to coach me, so, when the meet day came, I was left to my own devices.

Standing there among the other boys, who were mostly clad in Track uniforms, (shorts, spiked shoes, and sleeveless shirts.) I wished that I too had something more appropriate to wear besides blue jeans, a Tee shirt, and clod hoppers. I watched as the other guys took their turns, gliding across the 7-foot metal ring in a whirling motion and letting fly. It looked simple enough, but I would learn, shortly, it wasn't. Each contestant got to throw three times and the best throw, of the three was the one that counted. Needless to say, that with no training, no practice, no coaching, no technique…no knowledge of this event, I was doomed to failure. Needless to say, I didn't "throw it a mile." I didn't win, as I'd hoped… but I didn't come in last either, I was about the middle of the pack. I figured, just wait till next year.

Next year came, I was in the seventh grade, and this time, I had a coach in Mr. Ralph Grey. He showed me how to hold the discus and how to whirl across that metal ring and let the discus fly without stepping outside the ring. That year, I qualified to go to the State meet. Again, I didn't win, I didn't even place, but I had gone from someone who had never even seen a discus, last year, to someone who was throwing among the best throwers in the state, I was good enough to be there, and that, in itself, was an accomplishment.

School was out, I had graduated to the eighth grade, and Mr. Grey, the track coach, allowed me to take the discus home for the summer. I practiced throwing every spare minute that I had. I couldn't do it every day because I had to haul hay, mow grass, work for the town on the Green Thumb program, or anything else I could do to earn money. See, I needed school clothes, I needed spending money, I needed stuff, and back then, if you wanted something, you got up off your ass and earned enough money to buy it. Still, I made time enough to practice on my discus.

The following spring, track season came and I was ready. I had practiced with that discus on sunny days, rainy days, in the rain and even in the snow, I even threw it in my sleep. In practice one day before any of the scheduled meets had started, I spun across the metal ring and let one fly. This one was different. I could feel it when it left my fingertips. Maybe it was the angle of my arm when

I turned it loose, or maybe it was the speed across the ring, I didn't know, but something was different, this one was gonna go for that proverbial mile, and I knew it, instantly. As I watched in amazement, the Discus came to earth just beside the high jump pit.

"Did you scratch?" Mr. Grey yelled from the High Jump pit.

"No," I replied, still standing within the metal ring.

"Let's get out the tape and measure that one, He said, "It could be a good one."

We got the tape and measured from the metal ring to the point where the discus first hit the earth.

"One hundred, forty-three feet, nine inches, I think we've got a new record," Mr. Grey said with a smile on his face. "I'll have to check, of course, but I think it's a new record....in fact, if I'm not mistaken, you've just broken the Illinois State record, I think that it's a hundred and forty feet or so, I'll have to check."

"The state record is one hundred forty-two feet and eight inches," Mr. Grey said to me the next day at school, "Not only did you set a new school record, but you broke the state record by thirteen inches. Yours is not an official state record though, because you didn't do it in the state meet, all state records must be set in the state meet."

I didn't care, it was enough that I had set the school record, I had become Myron's Diskobolos in the space of a year. In my mind, I had taken my rightful place amount the ancient Greek heroes, I was one of them.

Later, after we had started the season of regular track meets, I would watch Mr. Grey as he would tell the opposing coaches, "I've got a boy who threw the disc a hundred and forty-three nine." As he said the words, he would smile, broadly with pride even though most of them didn't believe him. He was proud of me, I was a success story, for under his tutelage, I had gone from a kid who didn't even know how, to one who set the school record....and, for a while, the Washington Junior High discus record was farther than the Illinois State record.

In the last couple of days before I graduated out of the eighth grade and went on to high school, Mr. Grey, when addressing the student body about the future, used me and my accomplishment with the discus as an example of what dedication and determination can do.

As far as I know, no one has broken it, my record still stands, and fifty-nine years later.....I am still Diskobolos....

It was only the blink of an eye ago.

I was fourteen.

Hanging Drywall 1963

In the summer of 1963, I was 14 years old. I wouldn't see my 15th birthday until the coming November. I hauled hay and straw, mowed lawns, washed windows, even had my own shoe-shine chair in Downtown Eldorado. It would seem that I was quite an industrious young man and, I guess that was true. Back then, almost all youngsters worked, especially if you were Po' folks. Working was just something that was expected of you. If you wanted spending money, you worked. If you wanted new school clothes, you worked. If you wanted anything that cost money…you worked. See, back then Mom and Dad didn't just hand out money, like they had a big bag full of the stuff sitting in the corner in the living room, instead, they taught us to work and earn our own way. Back then, we didn't have food stamps, snap programs or food pantries, back then, we raised gardens and found something to do that would pay us money.

It was in this backdrop that my mother cooked up a scheme with my older brother, James, to get me away from some of the guys I used to run around with. I guess she thought that Earnie was a bad influence on me and was trying to nip it in the bud. The deal was that James would take me to Indianapolis for the summer and put me to work hanging drywall. I would live with him and my sister-in-law, Phyllis, and he would pay me $35.00 per week. Of that $35.00 per week, I would be expected to give Phyllis $10.00 a week for doing my laundry and cooking meals. The rest would be mine to do with as I pleased, as long as I had school-clothes at the end of the summer. I wasn't privy to this agreement between my Mother and Brother and didn't figure it out until sometime later in life.

The trip to Indianapolis was filled with chatter about the coming weeks and how much I was going to learn under the tutoring of my brother and his partner, Leo Braden. I was excited, to say the least, but still, I had that streak of cockiness that is so much a part of a youngster who thinks he knows the mysteries of the universe at the tender age of 14.

"Boy, can you drive nails?" He said, smiling as he anticipated my answer.

"Shoot," I said, displaying the cockiness for all the world to see. "Anybody can drive nails. There ain't nothing to it."

"In drywall?" He said, smiling, "and fast?" You know, you've got to be able to nail a board off pretty quick to keep up with me and Leo. You sure you can do that and not ruin the board?"

That cocky 14-year-old mentality driving me on, I said, "Sure, piece of cake." He only chuckled, looked at me and said, "We'll see, Hoss, we'll see."

We arrived at their house on Standish Avenue in Indianapolis on a Sunday afternoon. They lived in a duplex home, what we called a "Double," back then, that was owned by our uncle, Anuel Suits. After unpacking the car, James set about finding enough of his old hanging tools to outfit me for the work I would be expected to do. He dug up an old cloth nail apron that had seen better days. It had a couple of strings that tied at your back, and it was divided into two pouches in the front. The left pouch would hold a handful of one and one-quarter inch ring-shanked drywall nails, the right side would hold my tools. After searching further, he came up with an old, worn-out drywall hatchet, measuring tape, utility knife, and a pencil. All this would be kinda stuffed down in that nail apron so it would be right near my right hand when I needed it.

"When you nail drywall on," James was saying, "You put a set of two nails about sixteen inches down from the top and another set about sixteen inches up from the bottom, you can't break the face paper either, with the hammer or the nail. If you do, you'll have to put in another nail, either above or below the nail that damaged the face paper. The nails have to be driven straight in, too, and they have to be driven so that they are slightly recessed below the face of the drywall surface."

"Why recessed?" I asked, not understanding the concept, "Won't the nails hold it on the wall without the recess?"

"The recess is not about holding the drywall on," he answered patiently, "it's all about the finisher. See, when you spot the nails with drywall mud or tape the flats or angles, you don't want the wipe down knife to hit any nail heads, it'll leave a little ridge in the mud every time and it gets harder and harder to fix every time you put another coat of mud over it. You have to fix it the first time...you gotta think smooth."

It was a little more than I was prepared to wrap my head around at the time but tomorrow would be another day. Tomorrow, I would be on the job. Tomorrow, would be my baptism of fire.

Five a.m. Monday morning, came early. The tools of the trade were hastily loaded into my brother's work vehicle, an old surplus jeep, and we were off for the day. By this time, the city streets were alive with early morning blue-collar people, the ones who make America work. It wasn't the money people, they were all still asleep in their nice warm beds, it was the builders. It was the men in the trades who were out in force, traveling to projects all over the city, earning a living and building America...and at fourteen, because of my mother and brother, I was there among them.

We pulled into a housing addition on the eastern outskirts of Indianapolis, and after finding the house that was our job for the day, began the process of unloading all the hanging gear. There was, of course, the personal tools like the belts, pouches, and nail aprons, but there were others also. There were hanging benches, aluminum saw horse type things with adjustable legs. They would adjust to fit different heights in three-inch increments. They had a rail, midway up on the legs so that you could step up and onto the ten-inch wide top. They were like four-foot-long platforms from which you could work on ceilings.

There were drywall saws that were used to cut out doorways and windows, T-squares for large end cuts on the drywall and foot jacks for raising the bottom board up off the floor to close the gap between the top and bottom board. I was in for not only a bunch of hard work, but also an education.

James' partner, Leo, showed up and began to unload his own tools. Leo was a mountain boy out of Eastern Kentucky. Older than James by eight or ten years, what he lacked in youth was more than made up for in job knowledge. These two unlikely partners made a team that was more like a drywall hanging machine than just two guys that could hang drywall. The amount of drywall that they could hang in a day was nothing short of phenomenal, as 10,000 square feet per day was relatively common for these guys....and the days were usually about seven hours. Watching them work together, I could actually see the old saying "Poetry in motion" at work. It was as if each could read the others' mind. No sooner was one ceiling board fastened to the trusses than one of them would jump down, off the hanging bench, and start preparing the next board for the next cut while the other would stay up on the bench and take the measurements for the next board. There was never any lost motion. Every move was calculated to save time and get that next board fastened into place as quickly as humanly possible. I started learning how to hang drywall long before screw guns, screws, and routers were used in residential drywall. The use of adhesives was just starting and I wouldn't be involved in that till the following year. I didn't know it at the time, but I was going to be taught by two of the very best in the business.

For the next two or three months, my first duty every morning would be to unload the tools at the jobsite. Next, I was expected to strip the drywall, (remove all the little one-inch-wide paper strips on the ends of the drywall that held it in pairs), set up the hanging benches and just be around when James or Leo need something. In addition to these things, I was expected to throw the scrap out the windows or pile it up in one place in the floor, depending on which contractor we were working for. I was expected to watch James and Leo and learn the techniques they used in cutting and hanging the sheets of drywall. I learned how and when to use a T-square. I learned how to use a measuring tape and utility knife to accurately cut just the right amount off the ends of the sheets.... In essence, I was becoming a cut-man. This is not to say that I was a drywall hanger, at this point, I wouldn't have made a pimple on a drywall hanger's butt for there is far, far more to "turning it white" than knowing a little bit about how to cut. I was learning, though.

It wasn't too long before they let me start hanging some sheets by myself. I started in the closets, where anything I messed up wouldn't be nearly so apt to be noticed...and mess up a few, I did. It seems that the question, "Boy, can you drive nails?" was answered correctly when I picked up my hammer and stepped into my first closet. First, I drove the nail on my index finger, and actually left a small piece of the fingertip under the nail head in the angle. Next, was my ring finger nail, followed by my left thumb nail. I guess by the end of that first summer, I had successfully driven all the nails on my left hand, still, over the course of the summer, I learned the technique required to keep my fingers intact and to make a good job of the drywall. I could turn out a decent closet, but I was still woefully slow, the necessary speed, however, would come in time.

It is very doubtful that my presence on any of those jobs of long ago had any effect on James or Leo. They were doing just fine long before I came along, and after I had gone back into oblivion, they continued as if I had never been there. What they could not know, though, was that they had started a fire in the creative side of me that would burn until I draw my last breath. Learn to hang drywall, I would, and did, and in the summers that followed I learned to finish drywall also. It wasn't in me to be satisfied with just knowing how, that knowledge only makes one mediocre. I had a burning need to know all the little things, all the whys and why nots, that makes the difference between the commonplace and the outstanding. I wasn't afraid to try some new technique or tool. Knowledge of my chosen passion was my friend and I gathered all that I could find. Unknowingly, they had nurtured that creative part of me until the time that I was capable of going out and earning a living with my skills. It took years, with some breaks in the middle, but I got there.

In the end, I never was able to match the speed of my brother James. He was just simply too fast for me to match. On the other hand, there came a time when I could put my work, my finished product, up against anyone's, including James and Leo's, and not have to take a back seat to them.

At this point, I think it necessary to say a special "Thank You" to my brother James. Had he been a lesser man, had I done without his guidance, his criticism, his pushing me, I probably would have never made it to the ranks of "one of the Best."

Back then, James and Leo called me "Drifty."

I was 14 years old.....

My Rolls Royce

I saw a 1957 Chevy today, on my way home from Marion, and instantly took a trip into the past. I can't say it all, here, but there were a lot of good memories. My wife, Donna, and I did a lot of grinning, and a little laughing out loud. Seeing that old Chevy took us back to a simpler time, a time when life was much slower, easier. We spoke of the square in Harrisburg and all of the businesses and things that have taken their places in the past. We spoke of our hometown, Eldorado, and the downtown that used to be but, unfortunately, is no more. We revisited the movies, the drive-ins, the sidewalk sales, the eating joints, but I always came back to my Rolls Royce.

It was 1965, back then, there were bright street lights, businesses, and lots of people in downtown Eldorado. Back then, cruising the square, with a run through the Lotta Burger about every other time, was a must for most of us kids. 1965 was also the year that I bought my first Rolls Royce. Actually, it was 1957 Ford, but Rolls didn't have a thing on that car. She was mine, bought with the sweat of hanging drywall all summer. She was a four-door sedan, with an automatic transmission that had a leaking seal, and one of those cheap, black, Earl Scheib paint jobs. Even with all of her obvious and not-so-obvious flaws, she was the most beautiful thing that I had ever seen....and she was all mine.

I loved that old car, even though she kept me broke most of the time. She was on a liquid diet of bulk oil from the Martin station, transmission fluid from Cousin Fred's, and regular, leaded gasoline from whoever was the cheapest. She was my magic carpet, and she took me on many a fantastic journey. It was through her windshield that I watched as life, back then, unfolded. It was on her front bench seat, with my right arm firmly around some lovely young lady who had gotten in and scooted up next to me, that I fell in love so many times. It was in that seat, and behind her steering wheel, that I made so many trips around the square and through the Lotta Burger on all those long, warm summer nights. She wasn't very long, but she was my limousine, and she was all class, that girl, from that fuzzy thing that I put around her rearview mirror, to the slick vinyl seat covers, to the small blue bulb in her dome light. She had an AM radio that I kept tuned to KXOK St. Louis, in the daytime, and at night, WLS Chicago. There were no CD players, only her radio. There were also no plastic bumpers, no padded dash, no padded anything, except maybe you could count the door panels as padded...but that would be a stretch. No sir, her dash was metal of the painted variety and got its share of wax, just like the outside. Her bumpers were made of strong American steel and covered with mirror shiny chrome. Even the outside trim was real metal, as were the knobs on her dash for the radio, choke, and heater. She had ashtrays and a built-in cigarette lighter, and when we were young, we put them to good use. She didn't have an air conditioner, but there was no need for one. She had what we liked to call 2/70 air conditioning, that was the two front windows rolled down and travelling 70 miles per hour, and when you opened those little wing glasses, you had all the cool air you wanted. It didn't do much for your hairdo, but you were cool. On rainy days, you would turn on her vacuum powered, windshield wipers, and hope that it didn't rain any harder or that you didn't have to speed up too much. She rolled on fifteen-inch, nylon, whitewall tires, the kind that would "thump, thump, thump" when you first drove off on one of those mornings when the outside temperature had gotten somewhere down around the Brass Monkey stage, and the tires had a flat spot from sitting all night in the cold. They would "thump" until the friction of the road warmed them up. Every now and then, I'd have to use a bumper jack on her when one of those rollers would go flat. She had only two headlights in her front, but each bulb had a bright and dim that operated from a switch on the upper left floorboard. There were no key fobs back then and no electric door locks, but we didn't care. We lived in "small town" America. We left our keys in the car with the windows down and doors unlocked. Nobody even thought about stealing a car in our little community, it was just something that didn't happen. Her dash didn't look like the console of a 747 airliner; there was no need. We didn't have all the gadgets back then. Our AM radio, heater fan and cigarette lighter were enough. Under her hood, there was enough room to work on the old 289 engine that gave her life and I had to work on it on occasion.

The day finally came when I couldn't save her life any longer. It required skills and money that I just didn't have. Points and plugs, oil changes, used starters or generators every now and then were one thing but cranks, heads and overhauls were more than I had the talent for, I had to let her go, and she was traded for another.

I have owned many cars in my lifetime, new, used, all different makes and models but none had ever made anything close to the impression on me as that of my "Rolls Royce." Sometimes, in my mind, I walk out the front door of our house on First Street, out, across the sidewalk and down the little grass covered right of way between the sidewalk and the street. I push the button on the door handle and open the door. I slide into the seat, behind the steering wheel, and as I turn the key and start her up, once again I look at the world through her windshield, and I watch, as life continues to unfold....

She was a '57 model, and at this writing, it has been 57 years ago...

I was sixteen years old........

Marion

Back in the day, Jack Smith was my best friend. We went through Jr. High, and High School together, graduating in 1967. Jack, while in Jr. High, was a little on the chunky side. That little bit of extra weight would fool you though, because he was very agile and a good athlete. He lived with his grandmother and uncle in a white house on State Street, just beside the Skaggs Jeep Dealership.

From the beginning of our friendship, when I started the seventh grade at Washington school, Jack and I were very close. If you had a problem with Jack, you had a problem with me, and vice versa...it was just that simple. I suppose that there are other friendships that are destined to be of the same caliber as ours, but I've never actually seen one. Jack was family at our house, and I was the same at his. We worked together, played together, suffice it to say, we were almost inseparable. In the seventh and eighth grades, we were both starters on our baseball and basketball teams. It was the spring of 1963, when I set the school record for the discus, with a throw of one hundred forty-three feet and 9 inches, Jack was there. (to my knowledge, I still hold that record and have since 1963...almost half a century. My throw was 13 inches better than the Illinois State record at the time.) When we got to High School, and attended our first August football practice session, we were both hooked. Jack started as the center on the Freshman-Sophomore team, and I, as the quarterback, even then we were a team. After hiking the ball to me, Jack kept the defensive linemen and the rushing backs off of me while I went about handing the ball off, faking a handoff, passing, or just running it myself. It surely was a comfort to me knowing that Jack Smith was upfront in the trenches.

In our junior year of high school, we had won our first five games and lost one to Cairo. Marion was the next game and was hard fought. We were trailing by a point or two, in the last quarter, with only two minutes left in the game. We had the ball though, and we were steadily marching to the goal. It seemed for all the world that we would surely win, but then something amazing happened. Somehow, and unbelievably convenient for Marion, there was a power failure. All the lights on the football field, the scoreboard, everything went black. When the lights came back on, our momentum was broken. When the buzzer sounded, and we lost the game, we were within spitting distance of the goal line. We were upset, but there was nothing we could do but accept it and wait for next year.

By the time we got to our senior year in High School, Jack was playing right offensive and defensive tackle....and he was a terror. I was no slouch myself. I had passed our way to victory over our arch rival, Harrisburg, ran two or three touchdowns to win against Sparta, a new team on our roster, and on many occasions, faked a handoff so well that even the referees didn't know where the ball was and whistled the ball dead at the line of scrimmage, while I was rolling out to throw a pass to our end who was standing all alone in the end zone. Jack and I were still a good ream. The game that we had waited for, for over a year, was finally here. We had been dismissed from school early so that we could attend a pep rally downtown. Emotions were running high, and we all wanted revenge for last year's defeat. Back then, Eldorado was a Football town. Oh, when basketball was in season, she was a strong supporter of our teams... but make no mistake, Eldorado was a football town. At that time, there were only 3500 people in our little bustling community, but she was purple and gold through and through. People traveled, wherever our schedule took us, by the carloads, and busloads, to watch us play and cheer us on. Tonight, all the students were depending on us to win and erase the shame, the school was depending on us, the whole town was depending on us. In silence, we ate a very light supper and then, it was time.

Jack and I walked into the equipment room, holding our breath to keep the foul, thick odor of old sweat out of our noses and lungs. All, our pads, helmets, shoes, practice jerseys, and pants were hanging in the fetid, unmoving air of that closed up cubicle of stink. It was 6:00 pm, it was Friday night football in September 1966, and we were playing Marion Wildcats on our home field. Taking our hangers down from their places, we raced to exit the room.

"God Almighty," Jack gasped, "That room gets worse every time we go to hang up our gear up in there. It's a good thing we get to wash our game uniforms at home." "Don't forget the jock straps," I replied.... and then, "You'd think that they'd try to get an exhaust fan going in there."

"Naah," he said, in a philosophical tone, "that'd be too easy for the powers that be. They have to make something hard out of it before it's worthwhile. Besides, they're not the ones who have to walk in and out of it twice a day, five days a week." Satisfied that he had explained it as well as it could be explained, he turned to me with a twinkle in his eye, chuckled, and said, "Anyway, I would think that a fart sniffer like you would enjoy it in there."

"Screw you, Pig humper, and the horse you rode in on," I said, as he roared with laughter.

The team manager stuck his head into the locker and said, "Two minutes, put a move on it."

"Whack." Someone's wet towel hit the wall beside his head, and he backed out quickly with a yelp. The locker room rang with the laughter of youth.

Soon, we were on our way to the field. We ran across Saline Ave, up and over the practice field and then, we were on the track that surrounded our football field. Back then, we didn't have one of these big fancy facilities, like they have today. We had what could be described as a cow pasture with white lines and numbers on it, but it was OUR, cow pasture, and we loved it. Our cow pasture was separated from the track by a short chain-link fence that stood about three feet tall and sat about eight to ten feet from the playing field. The Player's benches sat inside that fence and the bleacher seats for the spectators sat on the track, and tonight, they were full. We crossed the track and ran onto the North end of the field to the wild and excited cheers of Eldorado's Faithful, our devoted fans. We formed a large circle, with Jack and I in the middle to lead, and we began our warmup exercises.

I had butterflies, I always got them at the beginning of a game. Everybody did, but with the kickoff, the butterflies disappeared, the adrenalin kicked in, and we were off to the races. Marion had chosen to receive the first kickoff and much to the dismay of the poor receiver, Ronnie Drone put one of those bone-crunching, pad-popping tackles on him that could be heard for the length of the field, and the tone had been set for the night. After three unsuccessful attempts to advance the ball, Marion was forced to punt. We took possession of the ball, and I began probing the defensive line for weak spots. I ran the quick openers first, the plays that sent the halfbacks straight forward, testing the defensive guards and tackles. These early plays proved successful and we moved the ball forward. Next, I ran some off-tackle plays, then one that sent our fullback right up the gut, (Straight ahead). It was time for "Old Reliable," the Straight 26 or 45 pass. This was a pass play that exactly mimicked the running play with the same number. In this play, I would fake a handoff to the fullback right up the middle, fake another handoff to the halfback going to the right, and then roll out to the left and pass the ball to the left end, who was hopefully behind the defender and on his way to the goal line. Danny Ramsey was there and waiting. My pass was on the money, and after hauling it in, he sprinted to the goal and six points appeared on the scoreboard. It was as easy as that. When I say "easy," I don't mean to imply that it was just the easiest thing in the world to score, it wasn't. What I mean is that everything worked according to plan, like it was designed to do. See, this was before all the new-fangled rules about not touching the Quarterback, or tackling head first (now called spearing). When the ball left my fingers, a lot of times I got my bell rung, real good, by some over-zealous defender who was just trying to put me out of the game. Later in the year, that's exactly what would happen, but that's a whole story. Halftime came and went with pretty much the same results. We weren't running over them, but we were comfortably ahead.

In the waning moments of the last quarter, the clock was ticking down. There were only seconds left. We were on their 30- yard line, and I was calling signals trying to get just one more play ran. 3...2...1, the buzzer sounded, ending the game. The sounding of the buzzer, though, apparently wasn't enough to convince a rather large idiot, the left defensive guard, that it was really over, and they had lost. I say that he was an idiot because he immediately stood up, jerked his helmet off, and loudly proclaimed, "Alright, you sons a bitches have had it now."

Now, see, it ain't rocket science. In the game of football, a very rough, highly physical, contact sport, you never just stand up, jerk your helmet off, (it's the only protection you have against getting a broken nose and lumps on your head), and challenge eleven other guys to kick your ass when they're already pissed at you and think you're stupid. No sooner had the words left his mouth than Jack put a stiff right hand from the boondocks right in the middle of the would-be tough guy's snot locker, and followed up with a left hook to the jaw that would have made Joe Frazier proud. As blood and snot sprayed from his nose, the idiot exited the game, helmet in hand, never knowing what had happened to him. The damage was done, though, and the exit of the idiot was the signal for the second game of the night to begin, the brawl.

We had us a fine ol' time. Jack had given the signal and the rest of us, with whoops and hollers, just naturally followed him into the next level of combat. Spectators poured out of the stands on both sides, swinging and kicking. Referees were trying desperately to keep from being killed, it was a melee, and all the while, the idiot was blissfully unaware of what was going on around him. We took some lumps, but we gave those guys much more than we took. Finally, order was restored with a little help from the state police. With the Marion boys sufficiently chastised, we allowed ourselves to be ushered off the field by the police and held in the dressing room until the losers were in their buses and safely on their way back to Marion.

While we were being held in the locker, a fellow Eldorado Eagle football player from days gone by stepped in with a big smile on his face. He was wearing a brand spanking new hat and topcoat, both had mud all over them. Smiling from ear to ear, he said, "I got a Referee!"

I've played in many football games, from high school to the army. I've coached many others, but this, was the only time that I was ever on a team that won twice in one night....

I was seventeen!

Ear Plugs

Stepping out of the mess hall, into the freezing night air, I pulled the collar of my field jacket up higher to shield my neck and ears from the cold February wind. Supper this evening, as every other meal here at Fort Leonard Wood, had been bolted down under the watchful eyes of Company D's Drill Instructors. You ate, but you ate as quickly as your fork would fly, and then you got out. There was no after supper conversation, no time to sit back and reflect on the events of the day, just a rather rude voice coming from somewhere under a Smokey Bear Hat saying,

"Are you finished, Trainee? Well, then, get our worthless trainee ass on up out of that chair and make room for somebody that might be worth a damn! Get up, dammit, and Get Out! Move, Move, Move!!!!"

That cold February air was actually good for us. It allowed us to focus on something besides our hatred for the Cadre. Those cheesy, overbearing Drill Instructors.

Walking back up to Company Street to retrieve my rifle, which had been left at the "Stack Arms" position, along with those of two hundred or so other soldiers, I reached into my left breast pocket for a cigarette. Lighting up the Old Gold, and drawing deeply, I exhaled the grey poison out into the night.

"Bastard," I muttered, to nobody in particular, and knowing that Sgt. Synder couldn't hear, "Sons-a-bitches won't even let us eat in peace."

I walked up the sidewalk, happily puffing on that Old Gold and letting my mind stray back home. I hadn't noticed the figure that was quickly walking towards me. Too late, the gleam of a faraway streetlight touched the Lieutenant's bar on the figure's shoulder....and then, I was faced with a dilemma. I was smoking that cigarette, which, being right-handed, I was holding in my right hand. Now, Military regulations required that I, as well as anyone else in the armed forces of these here United States of America, whose pay grade started with the letter E, must salute any Officer, in any branch, of our armed forces, and I must do it with my right hand, and I must do it first! My dilemma was this: I had a cigarette in my right hand while the officer was two steps away, do I try to switch hands with the cigarette, or salute left-handed? Trying to switch hands with the cigarette would mean that he would already have passed me before I could salute, meaning that I would have failed to salute an Officer. I reasoned that a salute with the wrong hand was better than no salute at all, so I snapped my left hand to the brim of my cap. The Lieutenant's hand came up in salute as he passed, and I had gotten away with it for about three more steps. "Recruit!" the voice from behind me was loud, firm and almost angry. "Lock your heels, by Gawd. Tell me that I didn't see you salute with your left hand!" Then the order came. "About, Face, you idiot. You're going to stand here for a while and practice saluting correctly."

"Yes Sir." I replied, and tried to explain my error.

"Shut your face! By Gawd, if I wanted any shit from you, I'd pull off the top of your head and dip it out....Now, SALUTE!"

"Yes Sir." I said. All the while thinking that I was going to jail, and not knowing that this was a super minor infraction.

After what seemed like an eternity, I was allowed to stop saluting. The Lieutenant, smugly believing that I had been sufficiently chastised for this insult to his honor, turned on his heel and left me standing alone, grateful that he hadn't rushed me straight to the firing squad.

Pulling my rifle from the stack, I went back to our barracks. I wasn't through for the night. I still had to clean my rifle, shower, shave, write my letters and make sure that my footlocker would pass a surprise inspection...all before lights out. Tomorrow was another trip to the rifle range.

"WHAM, BANG," the sound of the nightstick hitting the insides of a garbage can could be heard throughout our barracks as Sgt. Snyder walked up and down the hallway yelling, in his roughest voice.

"Get up, ladies! Get your lazy asses out of those racks! We've got lots of work to do today. We're gonna teach you ladies how to shoot! Now, GET UP! GET UP!"

The sounds of many feet hitting the floor could be heard as the building full of tired men struggled to come to life and not be the last one to get into PT formation...Five O'clock comes early to tired men.

Once again, in the cold, dark, pre-dawn hours of winter, we gathered on the PT field and went through the daily routine of Push-ups, squat thrusts, toe touches and the like, until some of the fat guys were ready to puke.

PT over and breakfast gobbled down like a pen full of hogs, we were marched up to Company Street and allowed to stand at "Parade Rest," while we waited for the day's instructions. Finally, after we had stood long enough to almost fall back to sleep, the sound of the door to our Orderly Room closing brought us instantly out of our sleepy stupor and solidly back to the land of the living. There, walking out to stand in front of us, clip board in hand, was our Operations boss, Sargent First Class Dean. Taking his place in front of the whole company, he silently looked us up and down. You could have heard a pin drop on a cotton ball. First, Sargent Dean was one of those individuals who demanded respect. He was a very large, very black man who made you wonder how the Army ever came up with clothes and combat boots large enough to fit him. He peered at us with those large eyes that were just under the brim of that brown Smokey Bear hat, from a face that never smiled. Standing about 6'6", he was almost a Goliath. After a minute or two, he began to speak.

"Listen up, do everybody be havin' they ear plugs?" The silence was deafening. "I say do everybody be havin' they ear plugs?" No one dared to utter a sound. We were looking at the executioner. "Alright," he said matter-of-factly, and then he went into his pigeon walk, back and forth in front of the company. One foot would just hit the ground, and the other leg would dip before the next step. That massive chin would move back and forth as if it were sitting on a large, thick spring where his neck used to be. "Alright," he said again. "When we be getting' to the rifle range, an' you DON'T be havin' you ear plugs...I'm knockin' yo dick in the dirt, then, Ima put you in jail." He was enjoying this speech as much as we were hating it, but he made the desired impression. No one would admit to forgetting their earplugs. Luckily, I had remembered mine. When we got to the rifle range, you could bet that everyone had something to put in their ears, even if it was a cigarette filter.

It was February of 1969....

it was only a moment ago...

I was twenty years old....

The Trip Over

The brown, vinyl-covered seats, on their metal tubing frames, reminded him of the seats on the old yellow school bus, he used to ride to Shoemaker School, eight years earlier. There were other things that were similar, like the windows and the height and width of the inside of the train car. Letting his mind wander back, he imagined that he could see the farmer in the driver's seat, shifting gears as he drove the busload of budding scholars up and over the hills of rural Hardin County. Who was that little long-haired girl who didn't like him because he was the new guy on the bus? She....and then, he was asleep. The rocking of the train and the clacking of the rails had conspired to end his trip down memory lane.

A little over a week ago, the 727 had touched down and rolled slowly to a stop on the runway that was flanked on either side by fifty caliber Machine guns and Anti-aircraft Guns. After a long trip that had begun in Fort Lewis, Washington, he was finally in Korea. His plane had made a short stop in Anchorage, Alaska, where they had waited inside the terminal. Seated against the wall, he had watched as a flight of soldiers returning home from Vietnam boarded another plane for the remainder of their flight home. As he watched, one of the war-weary troopers stopped, leaned against the wall and without a word, just stared at him, long and hard.

The trooper was wearing jungle fatigues that spoke of many days of hard use. His hair was blond, and looping curls covered his forehead. The wide, angular face had a somewhat pointed chin on which the blond fuzz had just started to appear. His mouth was set in an almost invisible, knowing smile. There was no hint of a smile, however, in his haunting, blue eyes. Only a chilly, empty loneliness could be found there. As he watched the returning trooper take the last draw of his cigarette, and step on the butt as he turned away, he shook his head and thought, "What must he think of us, in our Class 'A' Uniforms and spit shined shoes. We, who were not going where he had been!" ....and he knew that he would always remember that trooper's eyes. The call came to re-board and soon, he was once again in the sky.

As his plane had stopped on the runway, seat belts were hurriedly unbuckled and uniformed young men, anxious to get their first up close look at the "Land of the Morning Calm," clamored for the door. When his turn had come, he stepped off the plane only to be slapped in the face by a most God-awful stench. Instantly, he thought, "I won't survive thirteen months here if the whole country smells like this." Inside the terminal, while processing in, he asked an Airman,

"What the hell is that awful smell?"

Not looking up, the Airman replied with one word, "Kimchi."

"Kimchi?" he questioned, as though the word was much too small to explain the odor. "What the hell is Kimchi?"

"Fermented cabbage," the Airman had replied, looking up through wire framed glasses and with a smile on his face. "They mix it with a whole bunch of spices and bury it in the ground for a while, then, later, they dig it up and eat it."

"EAT IT?" he almost yelled, "You're putting me on man, nobody could eat something that smells like that."

"No, man," the Airman had said, "they really do, they eat that shit three times a day. They have it with every meal. Everybody over here smells like that, it's on their breath, and they sweat it out through their skin, you'll get used to it."

"I don't think I could ever get used to that," he had said, still thinking that the Airman had lied.

Processing into the country had finished and he had picked up his duffle bag and got in line for transportation to the 177th Replacement Battalion. This place certainly was different, he admitted to himself.

About the only thing to do in his free time...and there was a lot of free time as he waited to be reassigned to his permanent duty station, was to go to the Lower Four Club and drink, a challenge that he readily accepted. He spent a couple of hours a day in what they called orientation, a class where they told him things like, "Don't drink the water here, their filtration system isn't as good as ours, you might get a disease." Or, "Don't eat fresh vegetables here, they use human feces to fertilize their fields, you might get a disease." It seemed that everything that they said had a "Don't" attached to it. After a week of sitting around going to seed, his orders came down, he was headed south, tomorrow.

He was awakened from his sleep by the slowing of the train. The rhythmic, back and forth rocking of his car had stopped and now, the clacking of the rails became slower and much fore audible. Instinctively, he reached for the duffle bag that held all his worldly possessions. It was still there, and he breathed a sigh of relief. It was dark now. He had spent the last eight hours on the train, an old diesel job that should have been scrapped long ago.

The trip south had begun at two o'clock in the afternoon in the Korean Capital City of Seoul. He had been assigned to the 142nd Military Police Company, in the southern port city of Pusan, and had been herded aboard this train with four other GI's who had been assigned to other units.

As the train slowed to a stop, he picked up his duffle bag and slowly walked to the exit doors. Stepping down from the train, and taking his place among the other travelers, he ambled into the crowded station and searched for someone to give him directions or information about how to get to Hialeah Compound, where his new unit was based. Walking on, through the station, he came to a large set of stairs that led to the streets below. At the bottom of these stairs waited another soldier who was looking up at him and motioning with his hand for him to come on down. This other soldier had been sent from Hialeah Compound to pick up five "New Guys." Ten more minutes of searching for the other four and duffle bags loaded in the five-quarter truck, and they were off to their new home some five miles distant.

The city of Pusan was alive with people and lights, not so different from other cities he had been in. Neon lights were just neon lights, no matter where they were. As the little truck wound its way in and out of the atrocious traffic on the MSR, (Main Supply Route) he waited, patiently, if not apprehensively, for his first glimpse of what would be "Home" for the next year or more.

The truck entered Hialeah Circle, with its monument to those who had died during the Korean War, located in the northwestern part of the city. The final leg of tonight's journey was a narrow little two laned road, lined, on either side, with shops, coffee houses, and bars. At last, the little truck stopped at the main gate to Hialeah Compound. After showing identification and orders to the Military Policeman at the gate, the driver proceeded to drop his passengers off at their new duty stations. For the last time, on this warm evening in June of 1969, the little truck stopped in front of the Orderly Room of the 142nd Military Police Company, a new chapter in his life was about to start. After all the waiting, he was finally home.

He was twenty years old.

The Trip to the Boat

It was early evening on Texas Street, twilight, and the neon lights beckoned to all the world. "Come and see, Come and see." Marvin Crane and I were there, killing time before going to work. We were scheduled for Patrol Supervisor tonight on the Graveyard shift. Passing many GI's that we knew from Hialeah Compound, we spotted one of our own, an MP named Rudolph Cryzer. Rudy was Bohemian by ancestry, and unfortunately, American by birth...but he was an MP. So, like it or not, he was one of ours.

See, it wasn't that he was a bad fellow, it was just that he was a constant crybaby, a pain in the ass. Nothing ever suited him, the food was bad, no one here spoke his native language, the people were bad, he worked too much, it was always something. He spent most of his time feeling that he was being mistreated and misused because he thought, he was meant for bigger and better things than being relegated to being just a lowly MP. He was one of those guys that you just hated to draw as a partner.

He had two men with him who were unknown to both Crane and me, although, I had seen them go into the Top Five Club with Cryzer before tonight. They were both older than us, probably in their middle thirties to early forties, and were introduced to us as German friends of his who worked for the Shell Oil Company, doing some research. They had a boat docked over at the port and were here for a month or so. In our conversation, it was mentioned that we would be out and about town after midnight. These men spoke a few sentences to each other, in the German language, and then invited Crane and me to come by their boat, after we went on duty, and have a beer and some German Black Bread. Normally, this invitation would have been turned down, but this was the graveyard shift. With the midnight curfew, the streets would be empty and like almost all the other midnight shifts, nothing would be shaking.

Crane and I discussed it, one beer on the midnight shift wouldn't hurt and we'd get to tour their boat, no one would know, so we agreed.

Back at the barracks, before work, Crane said, "You know we can't let anyone know about this."

Chuckling, I answered, "I didn't come over here on a turnip wagon, I'm smarter than that." (This is something that I have questioned many times since then.)

It had never occurred to either one of us that it seemed just a little odd, at the least, that two Military Policemen, meeting someone for the first time, only two minutes ago, were now invited to tour a research vessel, docked at port and have beer and black bread in the wee hours of the morning, our mistake.

After returning to Hialeah Compound and taking a quick nap, we got into uniform, buckled on our web gear, donned our helmet liners and strolled out to Company Street for Guard mount. Personal inspection and weapons inspection over. We climbed into our patrol jeep and after relieving the gates, 051 ammo dump, Su-Yung Harbor and the rest of the outlying MP posts, Crane and I headed to the port.

It was about 1:00 a.m. when we rolled our little jeep to a stop in the parking area at the port. It was dimly lit, except for the one boat that sat gently swaying in the water to our front. I didn't know anything about boats, but I thought it was about eighty feet long. There were plenty of lights on this boat....and more antennas than an antenna factory. I wondered at the time "How many radios do they have on this thing?" I couldn't put my finger on it but I was getting an uneasy feeling down in the pit of my stomach. Crane and I slowly approached the boat and were met by the two men who seemed very glad that we had come and very eager to talk with us. Stepping from the dock over onto the boat, they showed us the galley. This was the kitchen of the boat. It was painted in light colors and the booth type seating arrangement was red, and reminded me of the small eating joints from the 1950's. The Galley was as far as our tour would go. Four mugs of beer and a small loaf of black bread were brought out by one of the men and set on the table before us... and so far, we hadn't seen any sign of another crew member. With smiles and toasts, we lifted our mugs and sipped the beer....and within four minutes, Crane was fast asleep. This was quite unsettling to me because Crane was a whiskey drinker, Johnny Walker Red was his drink of choice and beer was like drinking water to him.

Crane was one of those guys that didn't get drunk and pass out on a couple of sips of beer, something was wrong here.

We exchanged pleasantries for a few minutes and then they began to ask me questions about Pusan, and then, about Hialeah compound. By now, that feeling in the pit of my stomach had become a voice in my head saying, "Get out of here." At this point, Crane was blissfully unaware of what was happening around him and was no earthly good to me. At the beginning of the questioning, it broke on me like a thunderclap, this wasn't just common curiosity, I was being interrogated.

I could see it now. Crane was the ranking man, he was a Staff Sgt. I was only a Buck Sgt. They had drugged Crane thinking that I would be the easier of the two to get information from. I was an MP, I had a secret clearance and because I was an MP, and patrolled it every day, I was familiar with the whole city of Pusan...I would know WHERE things were, and WHAT those things were. At first, they asked simple questions, and I answered honestly. These were questions about things that were common knowledge. Everyone, in the whole world, knew the answers. They asked things like, "What is the basic arm of the soldiers at Hialeah Compound?" Or, "Are the Korean Soldiers at Hialeah well fed?" Then, the questions turned into something right out of a spy movie. "Where is the main power source located on Hialeah Compound?" "Where is the Main Supply Route to Hialeah?" "Where, exactly, are the missiles emplacements around Pusan, and what roads lead to them, what kind of missiles are they, and do they have nuclear capabilities?" My mind raced, "These guys have no business asking these kinds of questions, and they certainly have no business knowing the answers." I dummied up. To these kinds of questions, trying to look as honest and innocent as I could, I simply said, "I don't know," or, "I don't have a high enough security clearance to be given that kind of information." To others, I'd say, "I'm only a Buck Sgt, they don't trust me with that kind of stuff. At one point, one of the men got pretty upset as he was waving his arms in the air and speaking loudly, in German, to his partner. I can only think that he believed that I was lying. His partner cooled him off, however, the line of questioning resumed with the same results.

After what seemed like an eternity, but was probably no more than an hour, the questioning ceased, they became once more amicable, and Crane started to come around, a fact for which I was truly grateful. I made our excuses, trying to leave the impression that I had no idea what had just happened. I hustled Crane back out to the jeep as quickly as I could and was gone like a shot.

The night, the air seemed to clear Crane's head somewhat and he asked, "What the hell happened? I remember the guy bringing the beer and then we... I'm drawing a blank here. What the hell happened?"

"We're gonna have to talk, Crane," I said, trying to collect my thoughts. "You're not gonna believe this."

Picking up the mic I pressed the business button, the little prick 25 crackled to life. "Student Taxi, this is Student Taxi 1-0," I said. "We are back in service and proceeding to your 10-14, over."

"Student Taxi 1-0," came the reply, "this is Student Taxi, 10-4, Student Taxi out."

On the way back to the PMO, I recounted to Crane what had taken place while he was in never-never land.

"I'll tell you, Crane, I was beginning to think that we were in deep shit back there. You went out like a light and they started asking all these questions.....I don't know who these guys are but I think we need to go to the CO with this."

"Are you crazy, Suits? You know what'll happen if we tell the CO what we were doing down there? We'll both get busted back down to buck private so fast that it'll make your head spin."

"Look, Crane, this is important," I said unwaveringly, "You were catching z's. You didn't hear what was going on, this was no joke, these guys weren't playing some kind of game, they were serious."

"You're gonna get us busted for sure, Suits," was all he would say.

"That may be," I answered, "But this is too important not to report, besides, ain't that what we're supposed to do? Look, what if these guys are here for espionage or some shit like that? If someone blows something up at the Compound, and maybe kills some of our guys, whose fault would it be if we didn't say anything? It may not be anything at all...but common sense tells me different. I just don't think that we should take the chance."

"Damn, Suits, you're gonna get us busted."

The few hours passed slowly as we talked about the events of the night. The sun came up and with it, the realization that in about one hour, I would be sitting in the CO's office trying to explain my actions. I turned our jeep over to the next shift, went to the mess hall for breakfast and then started for the Orderly room and our Commanding Officer, 1LT, Forney's Office. Knowing that I'd have to talk to the First Sgt. Before I could see the CO, I stepped into his office and requested to speak with the CO.

Coming to attention, I said, "Sgt Suits, requesting permission to speak with the CO."

"At ease, Suits," he said, "is there something that I can help you with or is it a personal problem?"

"It's not a personal problem, First Sgt," I replied. "Although, it may become one for me shortly, I'd like to speak to the CO about something that happened while I was on duty last night." I was committed now, there was no turning back.

The First Sgt. eyed me, puzzled, and then said, "Wait here!"

Standing there, I could hear the 1st Sgt. speaking to the CO. "Send him in," Lt. Forney said. In seconds, I was once again standing at attention, but this time, I was before my Commanding Officer.

"Sir, Sgt Suits requests permission to speak with the Commanding Officer," I said, in my most professional voice.

"At ease, Suits, what can I help you with?"

I began to explain the whole thing to him, starting with meeting Cryzer down at Texas Street. At some point, early in my explanation, he called the First Sgt. in, told us both to sit, and allowed me to continue. When I was finished recounting my story to him, he sat motionless, staring at me as if in a daze. The silence was sitting heavily on my shoulders, I just knew that I would be a private tomorrow.

Lt. Forney seemed to stir, to come back from some far-away place, and without blinking said, "Well Suits...I believe the ends justify the means. Let's get CIC down here and see what they think."

"You did good, Suits," the First Sgt. threw in, "This is too serious to just let it pass. At this point, we don't much care about HOW you found this stuff out, the important thing is that you did, and that you came forward with it...Good job MP."

Within fifteen minutes the boys from CIC were in Lt. Forney's office armed with notebooks, tape recorders, and cameras. I spent another couple of hours in the CO's office being interrogated by our guys.

"I'm not too concerned with some of those questions," one of the new interrogators said, "some of them were probably just to get you in the mood to talk. Hell, everybody knows what kind of rifle we use. But some of the other stuff, like missile pods and such, that's a big no-no for anyone to be asking about. Do you think you could identify these guys?"

"From a mile away," I replied.

That evening, I found myself sitting in a CIC vehicle, a block away from the Top Five Club, with a pair of binoculars to my eyes. Seeing Cryzer coming through Gate #3 with his friends in tow I said, "There they are. Cryzer is the skinny, blond-haired guy with the green plaid shirt and brown trousers...the ones directly behind him, the blond guy wearing the blue shirt and blue jeans, and the other guy, wearing the black T-shirt and jeans, are the guys that were asking all the questions."

"Are you positive?" the CIC guy asked, "There is no room for error here."

"I'm as sure as I would be if I was identifying my own mom," I said almost pissed off at the question. "I saw them up close and personal."

The next day, while working a different shift, I went back to the port. The boat was gone, and I never saw those men again. It seemed that they had just fallen off the face of the earth. Even Cryzer was amazed. After I had ID'd the guys, he hadn't seen them either. They hadn't said good bye, thank you, screw you, nothing. They were simply gone. I never heard another word from CIC, it was like nothing ever happened.

Now that I'm an old man, I like to think that in that other place and time, I did what was right, in spite of what I thought the consequences might be. I like to think that back then, my devotion to my country and to my fellow servicemen helped me to play a part in the discovery, if not the outright capture, of a couple of communist spies. I don't know if this is true, but it's what I like to think. The only other plausible explanation is that it was a test, set up by my own branch of military, to test the reactions of our own forces when faced with things of a covert nature. I guess I'll never know the whole truth, but, still, I know that Crane and I didn't "Get busted," and I know what I like to think.

I was twenty-one years old.

The Birthday Party

In the latter part of May, in 1970, the morning sun found me sitting in a small Makoli shop just outside Hialeah Compound's back gate, Gate # 4. This shop was typical of most Makoli shops of the day. It was small, about twelve feet by twelve feet, and had been thrown together, hurriedly, with whatever materials that could be scavenged. The roof was rusted, corrugated tin, the walls, old grey, weathered wooden planks, neither had seen a coat of paint for ages. Inside the furnishings, small tables, and benches were of the same design with old wooden planks. Sitting on the two small shelves behind a small counter, were the establishment's wares, a couple of bottles each of Soju, Porta-ju, Jin-ro, and Chinese Bengal. The Makoli was kept in a large crock container on the dirt floor. Nothing was cold, everything was served at whatever the room temperature happened to be at the time it was ordered. There was no heat or air conditioning, no luxuries of any kind. You could eat in these places, as long as you kept it simple: Kimchi, of the Japanese or Korean variety, Ramen noodles, or Yaki-Mandu. If you ordered food, the proprietor would send out your order and then charge you a small service fee. They always tried to charge American Soldiers more because they thought all Americans were rich. Places like this arose because the people were dirt poor and did anything they could to make a living.

I was waiting for my Korean friend of six months, Son Won Sik. I had met him, and three other Koreans, in November of the previous year, at this same gate. I had been on duty and was working the day shift. They had come to my gate wanting to try their English on an American.

Today was the day that the Korean people celebrated Buddha's birthday. It was also my day off, so, Won Ju and I had made plans to go to a small Buddhist temple within walking distance of Gate #4. With me, I had a small cooler, just large enough to hold a twelve-pack of beer, (which I had been careful to pack before I left the confines of Hialeah.) As I waited for Won Ju, I toyed with a small dish of Korean Kimchi. This stuff was the real deal, unlike the stuff you find in the grocery stores today that is made for the tender palates of Americans, it would set you on fire in a heartbeat if you weren't used to it, and I wasn't used to it. It was early and Kimchi isn't what I would normally consider a breakfast food, but, when in Rome, you do as the Romans do. As I picked at my dish of edible fire, Won Ju arrived and after he had gotten a good laugh at my inability to eat this spicy cabbage from hell without drinking something, we downed a couple of shots of Soju and began our odyssey to the temple. It was a bright, sunny day and we had started it by nipping at the bottle. We were full of mirth and the contentment of youth, we were happy to be alive

Walking down the little road in the thick layer of brown dust, we took turns carrying the small cooler, the dust arose in a little brown cloud behind us with each step. After about a half mile we turned up a small, well-traveled lane that had grass growing in the center, much like some of the dirt roads back home. There were small trees growing on either side of this lane, giving very welcome shade to the traveler. This shade was welcome because, from this point on, the lane was all uphill. Stopping and sitting on the grass beside the lane, we opened and enjoyed a cold beer as we watched the other people make their way to the temple grounds. It was a joyous time for these people. Small shops were set up along the lane and colorful banners told where food, drink, souvenirs and paper lanterns and candles could be bought. The paper lanterns and candles were necessary, especially if you were a believer and had a prayer or two that you wanted Buddha to hear. I, was not a believer, at least not in Buddhism, so there were no paper lanterns or candles in my future. Everyone, I guess, except me, was dressed in their Sunday finest, the Korean people are fond of looking their best in public. The younger men, for the most part, were dressed in suits; the older ones in their traditional Grandfather garb, with their tall black, woven hats and their baggy grey pants, and the women in beautifully colored dresses with ornate patterns of butterflies or birds. There were dancers, musicians, and Korean drums, as if it was the 4th of July.. Everyone was happy. Stopping frequently, to watch some different entertainment and have another beer, we made our way to the temple, a very old building made of logs, bamboo, and cement. Red clay tiles covered the roof. I was told that these buildings were a thousand years old. I didn't go in, I had a few qualms about being half-lit and making an appearance in church with a beer cooler under my arm. It was a Buddhist temple, but it was a church to them and I supposed that they didn't much want a drinking man like me stinking up their church, besides, I was content to see the goings on from right where I was.

After taking in the sights and spending a little money at the drink vendors, I was down to my last two beers. I was tipsy, to say the least, but I could still reasonably walk without wavering. As I opened one of the two remaining beers, a man came to me requesting that I give him a beer. I had only just opened one and hadn't taken a sip so I held it out to him and said, "Sure, partner, here you go."

"Ahni," he said, and pointed at my last beer, making it plain that he wanted my last unopened beer. Now, I knew something about drinker's etiquette, and drinker's etiquette says that you never take another man's last beer. I didn't want to be an ass but at the same time, I wanted this guy to observe the rules, after all, it was my beer. He began speaking quickly in Korean and Won Ju was doing his best to translate. As near as I could figure, this guy didn't want a beer to drink, he wanted an unopened American Beer that he could sell, and he was irate because I didn't want to give it to him. When an American soldier first goes to any country on earth that doesn't speak the English language, the very first thing he learns is the cuss words in the language of the country he is sent to, I, was no exception. I couldn't speak the Korean language, but I could certainly spit out the cuss words and I knew them when I heard them, and when I heard the guy start in on the "Kay-Sikki's," I stopped him, right in mid-sentence, and told Won Ju,

"You, tell this arrogant little slope-eyed prick that I'll beat his ass all over this mountain. He can either shut the hell up or get his ass kicked, the choice is his." Won JU, not wanting us to get involved in a fracas at the temple, tried to downplay what I had said and the other guy started anew. I quickly set my cooler down and started for him. He must have taken a cue from my unloading anything that might have slowed me down, on my trip to his jaw, because he quickly jerked back and started to run. Now, in my alcohol-soaked brain, not only was I a world-class fighter, but I was also an Olympic sprinter and I gave chase. Running up and over the rock-strewn path that went over the bald, treeless top of the mountain. I watched as he ran. He was just simply faster on his feet than I, and I was losing the race. In my foggy brain, I was still determined to catch him, though, so I continued the chase. After a quarter mile or so, I found myself in the familiar grey world of Sin Ae Won. Unknown to me, the path from the temple went up and over the mountain and down, right into the middle of the orphanage. Within the space of just a few steps, I was beset by crying children, and you can hardly run fast when you've got little arms reaching, trying to hold you back. Quickly, Mr. Kim, a very kind man, and the overseer of the place, was in front of me urging me to stop. They had all seen us running over the mountain, had heard the angry voices, and knew what was happening. They didn't want me to get into trouble with the Korean National Police, so they quickly decided to stop me themselves. They let the other guy pass through and then blocked the path for me, thankfully, they were successful.

My love for these kids far outweighed any anger I might have felt for some stranger seeking to dupe me out of a beer. My anger quickly melted away like a vapor at the scene before me. Little crippled, maimed orphan children, tearfully begging me to stop. Their reaction when they thought that I might be in trouble, showed me that in that place, in their world, I was among the well-loved, and held a special place in their hearts that no one else could fill...I was, one of them, and once again, I was humbled.

It was only the blink of an eye ago....

I was twenty-one years old.....

Hold On

In the warmth of the morning air, the old bus chugged and wheezed its way up and over the steep hill, belching great clouds of blue smoke into the air around the narrow little dirt road. Reaching the bottom on the other side, with a "Clunk," the front wheels of the bus dropped off into a small wash out in the road, the result of a recent rainstorm, causing the old woman standing in the aisle in front of me to drop her basket of cabbage. I stooped down, as best I could, in the grossly overcrowded bus, and while others watched in amusement, I helped her retrieve her vegetables.

"Kom-Sum-ni-da," she murmured, quietly. "Cho-man-ae-yo," I returned with a smile.

The bus, an old-timer with a suspension that had been worn out long ago, was all the driver could handle. Adding to his woes was the fact that the bus company's policy was to carry as many people and their luggage as could be jammed, crammed, or otherwise fitted into every nook and cranny on the bus. Comfort was not a factor, there was no profit in comfort, only in paying customers....and this one had lots, of paying customers.

Early that morning, I had boarded the bus in downtown Pusan with my friend, Son Won Sik, and had begun the trip to his hometown, Miryang, a small town that lay on the banks of the Nak Dong River some sixty miles distant. I had first met "Won Ju" (A name used for Son Won Sik by family and close friends) six months ago the previous November. Won Ju was a student at Dong-Ah University, studying Silkworms. Although I was acquainted with his aunt, (his father's sister), his uncle, and his cousins who lived in Pusan, I had never met Won Ju's family, and so, we had decided that the first time I got a weekend off, we would make the trip, first, though, there was preparation to be made.

Living at Won Ju's home, were four siblings, his mother and father, and his grandfather. There were gifts to be bought for his parents and grandfather, but especially his grandfather. He was the Patriarch of the family, had his own room that no one entered without bowing, and even though his son owned the house, he had a say in all decisions that effected his son's family. For him, I bought two cartons of Winston cigarettes and a bottle of "Johnnie Walker Red." For Won Ju's father, I bought a carton of Winston cigarettes and for his mother, a box of Hershey candy bars and a box filled with various kinds of American can and box goods....and for his younger siblings, it was just American candy. He had one older sister and she received perfume. Needless to say, we had a load of our own to cram on that sardine can of a bus, and because the whiskey, cigarettes and American chocolate were hot items on the black market, they had to be watched very closely or some enterprising 'Slicky Boy' would have them and be gone before you could blink an eye.

Again, the bus lurched, but this time the old woman was holding her basket tightly. An angry bawl came from somewhere further back in the bus, accompanied by a few choice curse words in a language that I was only beginning to understand, Won Ju, laughed out loud. It was good to be away from Hialeah for a while. I was sure that I'd be ready to get back home tomorrow evening, but for now, I was glad to be away from the patrols and the uncertainty of what each day on duty brings. We had been on this bus for over two hours with stops at every mud hole in the road to let people off and take more on.

"How much longer?" I asked, wondering if we'd ever get there.

"Maybe.....one more half hour," he answered.

I was getting antsy, I wanted to be there. Standing in the tightly packed aisle of a slow-moving, rickety old bus did not make me a happy camper. Aside from being stared at by the people who were curious about Foreigners, I was tired of standing and holding on to the bags and boxes that we had brought with us, I was ready to be there now! That part about me wanting to be there, now, apparently made no difference whatsoever to the bus driver as he just kept on pushing the old bus at its apparent top speed of twenty miles per hour and purposely hitting every hole he could find in the road. He must have gotten some kind of twisted pleasure from making old ladies drop their groceries on the floor, or so it seemed.

Finally, we reached the bus station in Miryang, and after unloading, we loaded into a taxi and started for Won Ju's home.

"How much longer now?" I said, relieved that we were off the bus.

"Maybe, five minutes," he answered.

"Good grief," I thought, "why does Won Ju preface the answer to every question with 'Maybe'?

Reaching our destination, a small alleyway, not far from the river, we began the short walk to his family's home. He stopped at one of the many wooden gates in the seemingly endless maze of concrete block walls that lined both sides of the alleyway.

"This is my home," he said.

"How can you tell," I said jokingly, and laughing just a little, "all these gates look exactly the same to me."

"Maybe, I know my home," he said, without humor, "I've lived here many years."

Realizing that he didn't quite understand my sense of humor, I quickly added with a smile, "I was joking, I was joking."

The smile, if not the words, must have brought back the air of levity, for he smiled as he opened the gate.

Stepping through the gate to the other side of that endless concrete block wall, with its jagged, broken glass embedded in the cement cap, I saw a wood-frame house. The whole house was raised about two feet off the ground, except for the kitchen, which was at ground level and had only hard-packed dirt for a floor. The first room, with its sliding doors that were covered with oil paper, belonged to Grandfather. The second was the small dining room that doubled as a bedroom. There were two other rooms that served as bedrooms for Won Ju's brothers and sisters. It was, by the local standards, a rather nice home, befitting the principal of the local elementary school, Won Ju's father.

The first to appear was, of course, the man that I would later address only as "Dad, Son." Only slightly shorter than myself, he wore a dark suit and tie, an Ivy-league hat of the newsboy variety, and black-rimmed glasses. Clasping his hand for the first time, I was mildly surprised at the firmness of his grip. This man, I quickly decided, had no problem with self-confidence. I would later learn that Dad Son held a Black belt in Judo.

Next was Won Ju's mother. A smaller woman with graying hair, came from the kitchen to greet us and then quickly returned to the preparation of the coming meal.

Won Ju's brothers and sisters appeared, seemingly from nowhere. At first, shy about meeting an American, they quickly warmed up to the idea when candy, the international children's ice-breaker, was pulled from the bags. There was one brother, Son Kyung Sik, who wasn't there. Kyung Sik lived with his maternal grandmother in the nearby village of Wolsan. In Korea, the oldest son is responsible to take care of their parents when they get old so when the maternal grandmother had no sons, it fell to Kyung Sik, the second-born son, to care for her. He was probably only seventeen at the time but accepted the responsibility without complaint. I would meet him later in the evening.

Meeting the grandfather of the clan was a different experience, to say the least. Won Ju politely and softly knocked on his door and identified himself when "Noo-goh-sum-ni-kah?" was heard from inside. Won Ju then slid the door open, put the gifts on the floor inside, and only then did we enter, there was much that I didn't know about Korean customs. I had never bowed to another man, it felt strange, almost as if I was at a disadvantage. (Which, of course, I was.) Soon, the formalities and customs were over and we presented the gifts to Grandfather. He was pleased, to say the least. He would nurse those cigarettes and the Johnnie Walker Red for a long time, he would only bring them out for special occasions. We spent the rest of that day just talking. There were many questions to be asked of me and using Won Ju as an interpreter, we got through most of them.

Stopping for the evening meal, we all sat, cross-legged on the floor of the dining room, around a large table that only stood about one foot off the floor. On this table was placed a variety of dishes, from rice, kimchi, and spinach to baked fish and beef. I was surprised when Mom Son set a bowl of Ramen in front of me for fear that I wouldn't be able to eat the more-spicy dishes...probably a wise decision on her part.

During the course of the meal, I got the urge to go to the Korean version of the outhouse, so I politely leaned over and whispered into Won Ju's ear, "I've gotta go to the toilet, what do I say, in Korean, to excuse myself?"

With a sly smile on his face, he turned to me and whispered, "You say, Dong-noon-dah."

Trusting my friend to guide me through the unfamiliar territory of strict Korean courtesy, I put down my chopsticks, and rising to my feet, I said, "Dong-noon-dah," as he had instructed. Instantly, the room erupted in great peals of laughter. Mi-Ah, his younger sister, spit food across the table as she was unable to control the laughter. Mom and Dad Son, and Grandfather were all laughing uproariously. Apparently, and unknowingly, I had come up with a real knee slapper. I didn't know when I uttered the words, but what I had done was to stand at the dinner table of a family that I had just met, and loudly proclaim to one and all, "Dong-noon-dah," or, translated into English, "I've gotta shit!" Thankfully, this family understood that I wasn't well-versed in the finer art of Korean courtesy. I was forgiven for my colossal trespass, but, as you can imagine, it would be a long time before I would ask his advice on what to say again.

That evening, we went to a couple of Makoli shops accompanied by his brother Kyung Sik. Now and again, I would hear the words "Dong-noon-dah," followed by peals of laughter. I knew what they were talking about, they were getting every last bit of the humor from the dinner table. "You little prick!" I said to him. "Just you wait, your turn's coming." Again, the laughter rolled. I had been set up so completely that I couldn't help but laugh with them.

Morning came, and with it, the prospect of returning to Pusan. I was scheduled to work the swing shift, starting at 3:00 pm, and would have to be back by 2:00. That meant that if we took that rickety old bus back to Pusan, we'd have to start back by 11:00 to give us time to make it. The problem was that the next bus wouldn't leave Miryang until noon and that was just cutting it to close. We decided then, that we would take the train back to Pusan. The train was much faster, (and more expensive) but it departed Miryang station at noon, and we would be back in Pusan by 2:00. Now, I had a limited amount of experience with trains, truth be told, I had ridden a train only twice in my life, once, when my family returned to Indianapolis from Albuquerque, New Mexico, some ten years prior, and once when I first came to Pusan from Seoul. The train from Albuquerque went by American Laws and seating rules, the one from Seoul had been an express train which meant very few stops along the way, and no overcrowding. This train, however, had no such regulation. I was soon to learn that the same capacity rules that applied to busses...also applied to this train, get 'em on however you can get 'em on. The train was already loading, and in fact, was already loaded to the gills when we got there. It was standing room only, and only if you could find a place to stand. My place was found on the bottom step of one of the middle cars and by turning my back to the outside, I could hold on to the vertical bars on each side of the steps. This was to be my riding position for the next two hours.

I know, it was dangerous at best, but when you're young, it's almost as if you're unable to process the real meaning of danger, it's more of a challenge than anything else and not being one to just let a challenge slide by, (especially when the eyes of Korea were upon me, or so I thought), I stepped up on that first Sept, grabbed the bars waited for lift-off.

Lift-off came with the blaring of the horn and increased noise of the big diesel engine. Slowly, slowly, the train began to move forward on the track, just inches, at first, but slowly increasing speed until, finally, there was nothing to hear except the loud Clickety-clack as the large steel wheels of the train cars passed over the joints in the tracks. "Piece of cake," I thought, only a couple of minutes into the trip, but after thirty minutes or so I was beginning to wonder about my decision to ride this way. Could I actually hold on to the outside of a moving train for the two hours it would take to get back home? I hadn't given the tunnels a thought, either, but now, as frequently as we were going through them, I began to consider just how much room was there between the train and the tunnel wall. Was there enough room to keep my ass from being rubbed off, if I slouched just a little, not to mention the errant tree limb that might have been missed by the men who kept the tracks clean. Half way through the trip, I was tired. I wanted to be inside, sitting in one of those school bus-type seats, but this was what I had bargained for, and here I would stay.

Another half hour behind me and my shoulders were aching, numbness was setting in. I tried to move, as best I could, to keep the feeling in my shoulders, arms, and hands, a cramp, at this stage, would probably be an absolute disaster. The amazing thing was that in the few stops that the train made on its way to Pusan, no one had to get on, or off my car, and I dared not loosen my grip and lose my place unnecessarily. Over there, it was first come, first serve and sometimes, you had to hold what you had staked out.

Coming into Gupo, on the western edge of Pusan, I began to think that I just might make it back in one piece, and right about now, I was a happy young man to smell, in the air of that long ago Sunday afternoon, the sticky, tell-tale odors of civilization....it meant that I was almost home. The train began to slow down as it made its way into the Pusan Station, finally coming to a stop. I almost fell off the step as I tried to let go of the bars and jump down to the platform, but my hands didn't want to do what I wanted them to do. After a few seconds, grudgingly, my hands slowly began to do as I asked and I was able to free myself from the train.

We had made it back by 2:00. I was a little sore, for sure, but it would pass. Walking down the big stairway to the street below, we hailed a taxi, I would go to Hialeah Compound and get ready for work patrolling a city of a million people on the swing shift, and Won Ju would go to his aunt and uncle's home. That was, thankfully, my last adventure on a train. Looking back, I can truthfully say that I would never, ever try that again, nor would I ever recommend that any other cocky, full-of-himself young man try his luck at such a foolish venture.

This train ride happened in May 1970

I was young

I was foolish

I was twenty-one.....

A Day in the Life

A long time ago, in the world where I was younger, the sun broke over the T'aebaek Mountains like a big red rubber ball, shedding its light on the small formation of Military Policemen who were being inspected before going to their respective duty stations.

We were the 2nd squad of the 142nd Military Police Company, Pusan, Korea. As we stood motionless at attention, there on Company Street, Staff Sgt. Young, our operations NCO, was reading us the riot act because Larry Brighton had a small smudge on one of his spit-shined boots...or, Michael Gunn's handcuff pouch was in the wrong place on his web belt.

"Pay attention to detail," he droned, "you people represent my beloved Military Police Corp. You people represent ME! You people WILL, dress and act accordingly...Is that clear?"

As one, we answered, "Yes Staff. Sgt." The offenses were quickly rectified and the offenders were thoroughly chastened. Guard mount was over, and we broke ranks and headed for work.

Our duty vehicles were Jeeps, small, plain, OD green, four-wheel drive Jeeps. They had two seats in the front, two rear fender wells in the back, and on the fender well behind the driver's seat was mounted a PRC 25 radio, (We called it a Prick 25) our lifeline to help, if we needed it, information, if we needed it....and sanity, if we were patrolling alone, far out in the hinterlands. Slightly behind and centered between the two front seats was mounted the pedestal that held our M-60...that much-loved machine gun of long ago. Our Jeeps had red lights and sirens, a five-gallon can of Gasoline mounted above the rear bumper, and a strip painted between the hood and the windshield that proclaimed to the world that the 142nd MP was here.

Our duty dress was always the same. OD green fatigues with trouser legs bloused above highly spit-shined boots. A bright green ascot was worn about the neck and tucked into our shirt fronts. A web belt, that held a night stick, a handcuff pouch, a first aid pouch, an extra ammo pouch, and what Sgt. Young always called 'The Death Angel,' a 1911 model, Colt Automatic Pistol, with its holster was worn around our waists. Attached to the handle of that pistol was a white lanyard with a loop that our right arm went through, it was held in place by an epaulet strap on our shirts. A silver whistle hung from a chain that was fastened to the button of our left breast pocket. The black Brassard with the large white 'MP' just under the little red and white 'Eighth Army' patch, was worn on our upper left arm. Finally, on our heads rested an OD green helmet liner with the white 'MP' painted on the front and the 142 on the sides....it was in this uniform that we tackled whatever came our way, day after anxious day.

In the stillness of this Wednesday morning, I began checking my radio with the MP desk. As a buck Sgt., and one of the more experienced guys in the outfit, I never worked at the gates anymore, only mounted patrols, so radio checks were an everyday thing to me. Picking up and keying the mic, I began....

"Student Taxi 1-0, this is Student taxi, over."

"Student Taxi, this is 1-0, commo check, over."

"We hear you loud and clear 1-0 over," came the reply.

"Roger Student Taxi, this is 1-0, out." My lifeline was working fine, so I headed downtown.

I was alone today. We were always shorthanded, but that just meant that I wouldn't be spending the day babysitting some new guy, thank goodness. I pulled the little jeep away from Gate #1 and headed towards Hialeah Circle, about half a mile distant. Winding down the narrow little street, I passed the small Makoli shops, tea Houses, restaurants, and bars that lined the street with no sidewalks. Overhead was the giant, continuous spider web that some called electric wires. Why everything hadn't burned to the ground, long ago, I had no idea. As I approached Hialeah Circle, the Prick 25 crackled to life once more.

"Student Taxi 1-0, this is Student Taxi, what is your 10-14, over."

"Crap," I thought, as I picked up the mic again, "can't they leave me alone for just a few minutes?" Keying the mic, I quickly answered their question about my location. "Student Taxi, this is 1-0, Hialeah Circle, over."

"1-0," the reply came. "Be advised that we have a disturbance at Billet Juliet 27 on Hialeah Compound. Get there ASAP, it's a red light run, over."

"Can't the guys on P-1 handle this?" I asked. "They ARE compound patrol."

"They're busy on a resupply run," the answer came. "Besides, we don't want new guys on this one." There was a brief pause and then came, "There's a body involved. P-2 will back you up. Secure the scene and wait for CID, Student Taxi, out."

Pushing my little Jeep to its mechanical limits, I made my way back to the post, and Quonset hut J-27. Seeing P-2 roll up closely behind me, I bailed from my jeep and palmed the 'Death Angel.' I pulled the slide to the rear, and let it go. The metallic "Clack" of the closing bolt told me that 212 grains of instant death were in the chamber and waiting on me to say GO! The air was almost electric. I could feel it on my skin. I almost expected lightning to strike with my next step. Seeing the front door standing wide open, almost as if inviting me in, I dreaded the next few steps that would take me into....I had no idea what. Knowing that I must go in, and with Tom Agar and Mike Gunn on my heels, I let Mr. Colt lead, and drawing a deep breath, I reluctantly and cautiously stepped inside.

Mr. Colt swung, first this way, then that, trying to protect me. Mr. Colt was good. He had that ability to make 'would be bad guys' piss their pants just by looking at them. I trusted Mr. Colt. I took care of him, and he took care of me. The unmistakable odor of incense and cheap whisky hit me in the face as I stepped in, and there, sitting on a foot locker, the Army's versions of a place to store all your earthly possessions, was a black Staff Sgt., with eyes wide open in fear and disbelief. With tears streaming down his almost pleading face, he was wringing his hands and moaning pitifully as he mumbled unintelligible syllables. To my great surprise, he offered no resistance of any kind as Agar cuffed him.

Stepping deeper into the dingy, dimly lit room, I saw what appeared to be a statue, kneeling on the bed in front of me. The moment was surreal, nothing about this was natural, still, I moved closer. There, in front of me, was a young Korean woman, kneeling in an upright position...and held there by a curtain-cord that had been tied around her neck.

She was wearing a short, light green, sleeveless dress, with a beautiful yellow and red floral pattern and silver trim. Her hands hung loosely at her sides, palms up. Her head was tilted slightly forward as if she was in the act of nodding. Straight, shoulder-length, jet-black hair hid the ropes, until you got close enough to see. Her face had turned a bit yellow and blue-green where the blood had settled and her partly opened eyes had blood on the lower lids. It was almost as if she was crying tears of blood. There was no sound, no breeze, no movement...only this dead girl, hanging motionless, seemingly suspended in time. Yesterday, she had been alive, and in life, she had been beautiful. Today, tragically, she was gone.

We secured the scene, taking care not to touch anything important or destroy any evidence, and waited for CID. They came, took our statements, and began their own investigation. I cleared Mr. Colt, put him away, and headed for my Jeep, what a way to start the day. I can remember no emotion at the time. No sympathy, no pity, no sadness, nothing, not even anger. This was my first encounter with violent, unnatural death, sadly, it would not be my last.

It was determined to be a suicide. The Staff Sgt. was nearing the end of his tour and was scheduled to rotate back to the states. She had been his girlfriend and desperately wanted to go "Stateside" with him. He couldn't take her. She waited until he had night duty and while he was away, she got up on the bed, knelt down, tied the curtain cord around her neck, and took a bottle of pills. When the pills put her to sleep, she slumped, and the curtain cord hung her. He found her that way when he came home from his shift on duty.

More than a half-century has passed since I walked into that darkened room 9000 miles from home, and I still think of that beautiful girl who must have thought that she had nothing left to live for. I still wonder if I should be ashamed of my lack of emotion, my lack of feeling for another human being who died so tragically....so needlessly. There would be other times when tragic, unnatural death would touch my life, and, these other times, which were yet to come, would leave their own scars on my heart and mind....

I was twenty-one.

Texas Street

On June 23rd, 1970, the early morning Pusan air was stagnant, still, and heavy with the smell of asphalt and civilization. The mist, rising from the ground, hung in the air like dust on some old gravel road after the passing of an old, errant truck. It was 6:05 a.m. and we had just finished the ceremonious flag detail, where the American flag and the Korean flag were raised to their proper places at the tops of their respective poles, the national anthems were played and salutes were given. As Michael Gunn, my partner for the day, and I, strolled back to our patrol Jeep, the Provost Marshall, the boss of all Military Police Personnel in Pusan, leading a small following of C.I.D. personnel stepped out of the post headquarters building and walked over to my ride.

"Suits," he said, "I want you and Gunn to come with us this morning."

"Yes sir," I replied, as my right hand completed its hasty salute.

"We're going down to Texas Street," he said. "There's an individual down there that we've been trying to apprehend for a long time and our sources tell us that he's in a room at the Bayside Bar."

Taking a photograph from the folder that he carried in his hand, he said, "Take a good look at this guy. His name is Johnathan Baily, he's a Spec four, he's AWOL, and he's been selling government weapons and clothing on the black market. I don't want any mistakes on this one. We want this little prick...I, want this little prick." And then, he added, "We will not let him get away, understood?"

"Yes sir," I said, as he abruptly turned and walked away.

Texas Street was located in a part of town that was officially known as Cho-Rang Dong and was one of the many, and popular, red-light districts in the city. It was more like any alley than a street. Being only about twenty-five feet from bar front to bar front, there was only room for one vehicle at a time with the pedestrian traffic. Every door, on either side of the street, for three blocks, was a bar, and every evening, seven days a week Texas Street was alive with sinners from every walk of life. Beer, whiskey, and other worldly pleasures flowed like the waters of Niagara in this pit of debauchery. Texas Street was a colorful place, if nothing else.

There was the Tiger Lady, the female Martial Artist who was there because she liked it, you didn't choose to pay for her favors, she chose you. There was sweet Linda, (Most of the women there called themselves by American names because most of their business was from Americans.) She didn't want to be there but had no choice. Her parents, being dirt poor, had sold her into prostitution. There was Sim-So and Georgie, slicky boys who made their living there by bouncing troublemakers out of the area. Patrols and duty took us there, daily, and we befriended them all.

At this time of the morning, Texas Street, except for a few people walking back and forth to jobs in other parts of the district, would be empty. She lived by night and the sun never rose on the people who lived and worked here. The short three blocks of empty street were like a canyon where sound magnified.

My partner, Michael Gunn, was a rather large, slow-talking individual from Alabama. He had curly blond hair over black-rimmed glasses and a boyish face, there was nothing boyish, however, about the thickness and width of his shoulders, or the fists that looked more like hams, dangling at the ends of his arms. He was all man and I was glad that he was riding shotgun with me today. We saddled up and fell in line behind the boss's vehicles, winding down the narrow road out of Gate #1 towards Hialeah Circle. The little street finally gave way to the six lanes of the Main Supply Route that started at Hialeah Circle and ran for several miles to Yong-Do Island.

"I wonder why he wants us?" Gunn said, in that slow southern drawl. "He's got plenty of people in C.I.D., he don't need us."

"I have no idea," I responded, shaking my head back and forth. Pulling a cigarette from my pack of Old Golds', I lit up and blew the first long puff out into the already humid, sticky city air. "Sounds like he wants this guy pretty bad," I said. "We'd best be on our toes this morning...whatever it is that we're going into."

"Huh," Gunn snorted, with a half grin on his face. "I'm always on my toes." And with that, he clammed up.

Pulling into an alley a couple of blocks from the Bay-side, we formed a tight little knot around the boss. Once again, he passed the photo around as he explained what was going to happen.

"Look," he was saying, "we all know that there's a stairway inside that goes up to the sleeping rooms. When we get inside the bar, you and you," he said, pointing at two of his 'desk' people, "will come with me. We're gonna go up and catch the bastard asleep." "You three," he continued, pointing at the other three guys, "will stay in the bar in case he gets by us. Suits, you and Gunn station yourselves at the front and back. You don't let anyone out until you see my smiling face telling you that it's OK. We'll let you and Gunn get in place before we move in. Now, boys, don't let this guy get away, it's important....DO YOU UNDERSTAND?"

"Yes sir," we all agreed. As we began walking up the dirty little street I turned to Gunn and asked, "You want the front or back?"

"Don't make nary bit of difference to me," he drawled, "He's not gonna come out without handcuffs on anyway, like the chief says, he's bottled up."

"OK then," I said grinning, "Then I'll take the front. The criminals always run out the back door you know."

We took our places and Lt. Head and his boys entered the bar. I stood, wondering how long it would take for the guys inside to finish up. As I stood in thought, there was a loud crash as a small door just to the right of me burst open and Johnathan Baily emerged not ten feet from me. None of us was aware of the hidden second stairway that was only used in case of emergency. Someone had tipped him off that we were here and, unseen, down he came. I was caught completely off guard, and seeing me, he ran to my left.

"Halt," I yelled as I pulled open the flap of the holster that held instant death. Palming my pistol, I pulled the slide to the rear, and letting it go, I heard the audible "Clack" as the bolt closed on one of those big .45 caliber rounds....in that echo chamber that was early morning Texas Street, he had to hear it too.

"Halt," I yelled for the second time as I swung to bring him into my line of sight.

"Lord," I prayed, "please, make him stop; I don't want to shoot this man."

My mind raced, voices from my instructors back at Fort Gordon were running through my mind in milliseconds. "Don't let him get away." "Deadly force is authorized to stop a fleeing felon, hell, he hadn't even been charged yet, how could he be a felon." "Yell Halt, three times then pull the trigger. Never shoot to wound, this is real life, not the movies, always shoot center mass."

"Halt," I yelled, for the third and final time as I leveled the sights of that big pistol on a spot between his shoulder blades and tightened my finger....

"Please, stop," I whispered in desperation, "I don't want to kill you."

I still don't know if I would have, or could have pulled the trigger on another American...but that's OK. Thankfully, on that hot, muggy Tuesday morning, in another place and time, I didn't have to make that awful choice. I will always believe that the Lord heard my silent prayer, for Baily stopped in his tracks and I wasn't forced to make that dreadful decision. I hollered for Gunn, who had already heard the commotion and was on his way. We were cuffing Baily when Lt. Reed came out of the bar. He gave us a lot of 'Attaboys' and told us what a great job we had done. I didn't hear much of it though, for I was in a battle that was being fought in my mind. It's sad, but true, that the things that are imprinted on the fabric of a young man's mind, aren't always things of a pleasant nature.

I would be back on Texas Street tonight, out of uniform, where I would get stone, stupid drunk and catch a ride home with the MPs on the swing shift. This had already started out to be a bad day.

I was twenty-one............

Too Late

Standing beside the gurney, pencil and notebook in hand, I wondered, why? There were a lot of whys in my mind just now; like why did the Desk Sgt. send me here? This guy couldn't tell me anything. Why didn't the doctor just tell me that the guy was on his way out, that they had pumped his stomach, but too late, much too late? It would've made things easier for me. As it was, I would have to try to piece things together to make my report, nobody here knew anything. The trouble with that was that the "powers that be" wanted facts, cold, hard facts, not pieces. My report would be part of the official record and must contain only what happened.

The MP Desk had sent me to the 11th EVAC. Hospital, on Hialeah compound, to investigate a report of a drug overdose. The Hospital was required to notify us in the event of any injury resulting from suspected, or known, illegal activity. The Hospital had called, and here I was, doing my job. It was supposed to be simple. I had strolled in, told the pretty, white-clad Korean nurse why I was here, and was led to a room in the back where those white curtains, that hang on the tracks in the ceiling had been pulled around a guy on a gurney. It was like you see, sometimes in a movie. There stood the doctor, a perfect Norman Rockwell painting, in his long, white medical frock, stethoscope dangling from his neck and clipboard in hand, going over whatever medical stuff that was written down on his board. I identified myself, told him why I was here, and asked if I could ask the patient a few questions.

"Well," the doctor says, "You can ask all the questions you want…but I doubt if you'll get many answers," and with that, he turned, and walked away, shaking his head.

I pulled the curtain back and went to the guy's bedside, still wondering what the hell the doctor had meant by his comment. Pencil and notebook at the ready. I looked down into the face of an unconscious 18- year-old PFC.

"What the hell?" I thought as the realization of what the doctor had said broke over me, "How am I supposed to interview an unconscious man?"

Our line of questioning was always based on what we called "The Five W's," Who, What, Where, When and Why. The first four of these were fairly simple to obtain, I could get these from his company's roster, the CQ's report, and the hospital record. The last W, the Why, was the most difficult and only he could say, but he couldn't say.

As I stood beside him there, I began to realize that we were not alone. There were three of us there, PFC. Jacobs, myself, and the Reaper, PFC. Jacobs was dying. The shock of it broke over me like a wave of cold water on a hot humid summer day. I was standing beside someone who was in the embrace of The Reaper, and unknowingly was stepping into eternity.

My mind journeyed back, over the thousands of miles of deep blue water; I went home again. I thought of my younger brothers, Gary, Joe, and Marty, and my eyes filled with tears, but for the Grace of God, it could have been one of them lying on a gurney somewhere, for the same reasons. I had a praying mother, probably the reason that her boys didn't get into too much trouble. She had laid up a lot of mercy for us with her very frequent conversations with The Master, a fact for which I was truly grateful, especially, now.

A movement from the gurney brought me back to the emergency room in Korea, a leg had shaken, and then his whole body quivered, he was going into convulsions. Helplessly, I stood and wondered, "What could I do to help him?"

Death was no stranger to me by now, I had seen it, messy, clean, expected, and unexpected, but always before it had come, before I got there or after I left. This time, I was present and in the front row when The Reaper came to perform his grisly task.

Why? The question still clung in my mind. Why would any young man just take something that, in large enough quantities, could and would, kill them? This wasn't like drinking beer to get a buzz. This was a whole new ballgame. What would make him do such a thing? Was life that bad? Did he even know what the consequences could be? Why did he do this to himself?

Again, convulsions racked his body, his back arched, slightly and his left arm fell off the gurney. An object had fallen from his pocket and I picked it up. It was a small film container that once had held a new roll of 35 mm camera film, now, however, it contained poppy seeds.

"What a waste," I thought to myself, as I stood beside him there, watching him die. "Who knows what this young man could have accomplished in the years to come? His life, no doubt, would have involved a wife, children, grandchildren, the proverbial house on the hill, who knows? Now, instead, he had chosen to take the drugs that would put an end to all the speculation...by his own hand, he has ended the dream."

I felt hot tears well up in my eyes...not because I was squeamish, but because even though I had been somewhat hardened by my job and environment, the labors of my mother weren't entirely lost on me, and I still had sympathy for others in my heart.

Again, he convulsed. The pungent odor of feces filled the air as his bowels opened up. He pissed his pants as his bladder emptied for the last time...one long, rattling exhale, and as those hot, salty tears dripped off my chin and moistened my shirt front, he slipped away forever.

I had never felt so useless, so unnecessary. I could do nothing except watch and shed a tear, as one of ours died. I had no medical expertise beyond basic first aid, but even if I had been the most skilled of physicians, I couldn't have helped him. He needed a miracle that mortal men aren't capable of. In spite of all the sorrow, though, I was glad that I was there, because, maybe my being there wasn't because the MP Desk Sgt. had sent me. Maybe it wasn't about reports and facts after all, maybe a higher power had sent me...because my being there, meant that he didn't have to die alone.

I think of this day of long ago, often.

I was Twenty-two.

Because I Loved Them

Standing patiently in line and waiting my turn to get paid, I went over my plans to paint the town red tonight. I had only been allowed to go outside the perimeter wall while on duty. I had only been at my new home, in Pusan, for two weeks and today was the day that my restriction to the post would be lifted. I had seen many places during the last couple of weeks, but only in passing. I was in training or the acclimation period, as they called it, and wasn't allowed to stop and gawk. I had to learn the layout of the city. Tonight, though, I would be free to go and the first place I wanted to see was Cho Rang. The guy ahead of me shuffled forward and mumbled something about how long it was taking. I was just happy that I'd have a little money in my pocket and could finally leave the compound.

After what seemed like an eternity, the line had moved enough that I was now standing at attention before the Company Commander, Lt. Richard M. Forney. It was my turn.

Lt. Forney was sitting at a card table that held the company's payroll for the month. Standing behind and just to the left was our operation Sgt., SFC Amburg. Sgt. Amburg was armed with a .45 caliber pistol.

"Sir," I said, snapping my open right hand to the end of my eyebrow in a salute, "PFC John M. Suits reporting for pay."

"At ease, Suits," he said without looking up as he hunted for my name on the Company Roster, "Got big plans for tonight?"

"Yes sir, a few."

Handing me something in the neighborhood of a hundred and forty bucks, he said, "Put your John Hancock on the dotted line," and then with a knowing smile and a shake of his head, he added, "When you get down to Cho Rang, don't spend it all in one place."

"Yes sir," I replied once again, wondering how he knew where I was going. I guess he'd seen enough new guys to know exactly what they were thinking. Taking my money, I proceeded past the other card tables that had been set up to collect donations to various charities like the Red Cross and March of Dimes. Down at the last table sat a guy who had befriended me when I first came to Pusan, John Daly. "What in the world are you collecting for, John?" I said.

"Sin Ae Won," he answered.

"OK, I give up," I said, "What the hell is a Sin Ae Won?"

"It's our orphanage, didn't you know that we have an orphanage? Well, it's not really ours, but we sponsor it. In fact, we're the only support they get outside of a few individuals who contribute privately. See, the government doesn't really do much for them because they'll never contribute much to society."

"I had no idea of any orphanage," I said, "Why can't they contribute to society?"

"They're all victims of birth defects or accidents, or something," he said, "some can't walk, some were disfigured in fires, deaf, mutes, blind, you name it, you'll find it there." Taking a ten from my little wad of bills, I handed it to John. "When do we go?" I said.

"As soon as payroll is over," he replied, studying me closely. "But I thought you were going down to Cho Rang."

"Cho Rang, can wait," I said, "This is more important."

Catching a ride with a patrol jeep, we left Gate #4 and watched as a dust cloud rose up behind us while we traveled down the small dirt road. There were only a few rundown roadside shops on our way as we got farther away from Hialeah Compound, and the kids from the neighborhood ran after us begging for candy, gum, or money and were getting fogged by the dust all the while. About a mile down the road, we turned, to the right, up another small, almost hidden lane, that took us through a small gate, and into this mystery place called Sin Ae Won.

On the other side of the gate, and the sign that proclaimed to the world that this was indeed Sin Ae Won, was a world of grey. The dirt of the yard was grey, the concrete and block buildings were grey, and since this was an overcast day, even the very sky was grey. There were only three things that made this grey world brighter; the green leaves on the trees, the mismatched colors of the hand-me-down clothing that the kids here wore, and the bright white, toothy smiles of the kids themselves. I was instantly humbled, and I was instantly in love. Seemingly, out of nowhere, the kids began coming. Some walked, some were led, some were carried, some, literally crawled in the dirt because their legs were useless. But soon, our jeep was surrounded by smiling, beautiful, little crippled people.

At the sight before me, I wanted to cry out in despair and anger, "God, why?" My youth had not allowed me to understand the complexities, and sometimes the cruelties of our existence. I knew nothing of the oriental mindset. I only knew of the rage and sorrow that was building in my breast because of what I saw as the grave injustice of their circumstances. My heart was breaking, but I couldn't let them know. I hid my tears behind my own smile and decided that if I could, I'd make a difference in their lives. Somewhere, in the midst of all that emotion, the thought came to me.... "Only love them."

The two smallest were little girls named Ok-Ju, and Kee-ah. Both were only about four years old and both had been born with one leg shorter than the other. There was another little girl, probably six years old, who had been in a fire. Her scalp, on top, had been horribly burned and scarred so badly that only a few strands of hair would grow there...but this was not the worst. Her little hands were burned so badly that they were un-useable. The fire had drawn her fingers back towards the back of her hands. Her fingernails had turned black and now grew to look much like the claws of a dog, for all her disfigurement, she had a ready and beautiful smile. There were about forty or so of these forgotten waifs, each with his or her own story and each with his or her particular handicap.

Everyone worked at Sin Ae Won, everyone! Some worked in the garden that they raised in order to help feed themselves, it was seasonal but when they could, they did. Some worked in the laundry, some in the kitchen, but all worked. It was as though they understood that their existence depended on their cooperation. There were no shirkers.

The overseer of Sin Ae Won was a short, gentle, soft-spoken man of about forty, named Mr. Kim. Even he, was a cripple. His right hand was drawn up to the point of being almost un-useable. Still, he managed to conduct the affairs of Sin Ae Won in a satisfactory manner. He was much loved at the orphanage, and beyond.

The woman who ran the kitchen and the laundry was Miss Kim, (No relation to the overseer). There was nothing about her appearance that would make you look at her twice, although she was not an unattractive woman, she was just, plain. Makeup and flashy clothing were far removed from her list of priorities. The kids at Sin Ae Won came first, last, and always. She was very proficient at her job and went about it in a manner that drew the children close to her. She too was much loved.

My coming into the picture, proved to be a boon to the kids at Sin Ae Won, for I immediately began to organize activities for them, outside the "Grey World." I got some of the other guys in the company interested, like Miguel Zeta, who worked in our motor pool, before long, and for their first time, we were taking the kids, to movies on the compound, in a couple of our "deuce and a half trucks." They got to go on Picnics in the surrounding countryside and trips to some of their temples. Our trucks, and kind-hearted American Soldiers, made these things possible.

They had a large swing frame in their grey dirt yard, but no swings. I went to John Daly, he was in charge of supply at the 142nd Military Police Company. He gave me rope, boards, and paint. We made the swings and put a fresh coat of colorful blue paint over the drab, old, colorless frame. They had a back board for a basketball goal but no hoop, no net, and no ball. Once again, I went to John Daly. Somehow, he came up with not only a hoop and net, which we immediately put up, but he also came up with a basketball. The man was a miracle worker. Sometimes they just needed the simple things like soap, I got it for them. It wasn't just me, there were others involved...I was just the guy who put it together. It wasn't long before, I too, was among the "Much loves" at Sin Ae Won, and later on, during one of my escapades, they would show me.

I wrote a letter to my mother telling her about the plight of our orphanage and those little cripples that I had begun calling "My Kids." In it, I described, in graphic detail, the almost primitive conditions of life at Sin Ae Won. It must have touched hearts in my family because my sisters, Bonnie and Janice, took my letter down to the Eldorado Daily Journal office and had it published.

The response to my letter, in my hometown newspaper, was nothing short of miraculous. Before long, as the citizens of Eldorado and the surrounding area read my letter, the donations began to roll in. Clothing, games, crayons and coloring books, shoes, soap, every kind of non-perishable item that could be legally mailed came into my mother's house. People from all walks of life were stopping by 1209 First Street, holding out a box or sack, and saying to my mother, "Mrs. Suits, would you please send this to Mike's kids?" The astounding generosity, and compassion, displayed by the people in my home town, were almost beyond comprehension....and could only be matched by the selfishness and greed of the people in the Korean postal system. My mother had shipped at least 13 large boxes, packed full, and sealed tightly. The post office here had said that she must label each box with the contents. She did so, and the boxes were on their way. I never received the first box. The outpouring of generosity from my hometown to the children of Sin Ae Won was stolen at the entry port, (supposedly because the label told the world what was in the boxes,) and the contents were sold on the black market. My kids never saw the first crayon or bar of soap....and I never let them know, they had enough sorrow as it was.

Sometimes, I would help in the kitchen. Other times, I would help them clean. There were times when I would just be with them. We'd look at pictures in magazines or books...pictures of things that I knew they would never have, and places that they would never go, I would explain and describe America, (Through an interpreter) and show them, on a map, where my home was located. I took them to other places and times with my stories and they were willing travelers. My reward was always a gleaming smile with eyes that were seeing another place or time. For a while, as I wove a new tale, they were allowed to break free of their Grey World and step into a world of bright, vibrant color, a world where they could run and play as other children did...a world where they were free to be and do whatever they dreamed. I like to think that I brought them joy if only for a little while, for it is certain, that they brought much joy into my life.

In the time that I was there, I never heard the first complaint from one of my kids about the raw deal that life had given them. They were troopers, each and every one of them. They took each day as it came and accepted their lots as if that was the way it was supposed to be.

Much too quickly, my time there had slipped away, and in December of 1970, as the curtain of time began to close on that chapter of my life and my tour of duty, in the "Land of the Corning Calm," was quickly coming to an end, I went to see them for the last time. Little arms hugged me, and little lips quivered as they whispered, "An yung hee kah ship shio, Tom Sik," a Korean Good-bye....and as I caressed little dust-covered, tear-stained faces. They, for the first time, saw me cry and as my tears mingled with theirs, I whispered my own, last "Good-bye." It was because I loved them.

Very often, my mind travels back, over the years and I see little Ok-Ju and Kee-Ah, sitting on the hood of my patrol Jeep in their hand-me-down dresses and white leotards. I see the others coming to me, out of that grey world, arms outstretched, smiling in welcome. Where are they now? Did any of them succeed? How many are alive today? So many questions...

I still wonder, a half-century later, what became of "My Kids."

After all, it was only a few days ago,

I was Twenty-Two.

The Smartest Thing I Ever Did

Sunday, February 7th, 1971, was to borrow a phrase from a pretty popular Ex-President, "A day, that will live in infamy." It was my day off, and I was lounging in the day room of the 512th Military Police Company at Fort Huachuca Arizona. This day looked to be like all the rest, nothing to do, nowhere to go, but looks are often deceiving. I had been back in the states for only a short time and had been here for about a month and I really hated this place. I wanted to go home, back to Korea.

I had been placed in a line company, working as a traffic cop, mostly with people that I didn't care for. Van Dreece and Rohn were cops from LA who got drafted and now, they treated everyone they stopped as though they were enemy agents. They had a bad case of the "It's us against them," disease. And then, there was Robinson, the weirdo who spent entirely too much time in the latrine with his monster magazines. I didn't like these people and didn't want to be anywhere near them. There were others who were good guys, my roommate, Ron Triffen for example, the desk clerk, Tino Torres, and Bob Garza, but they were in the minority. The proverbial bad apples outnumbered the good guys.

The 512th was a chicken shit outfit. All spit and polish, from our shoes and Sam Brown gear, all the way up to the brass on our hats. Our duty uniforms were class A Greens, Khaki shirts with a black neck tie topped off with the white hat. Our trousers were bloused above the mirror finish of highly spit-shined boots. Our Sam brown gear, with its holster and various other leather pouches, had the same treatment as out boots. It was a far cry from what I was used to, back home. For months now I had worn a helmet liner, web belt and fatigues, green ascot, brassard, and trousers bloused above shiny boots. It was functional, it was comfortable and it was what I much preferred.

I had worked as the Desk Sargent a few times and disliked it immensely. Giving out parking or speeding tickets as a line cop didn't fill the bill either. I liked patrolling, being where the action was, I liked the freedom. I had come from having my own squad of people back in the 142nd to being a traffic cop who had to be careful who he stopped. I didn't like having to play favorites because of rank and that was the order of the day in this crap hole. There was no camaraderie, no esprit de corps. It felt like I had been demoted.

This day was just another sunny day in the desert, just seven miles from Mexico, as the crow flies. It was getting on about lunchtime and since I had skipped breakfast, in order to sleep a little longer, my stomach was beginning to think my throat had been cut. I got up and ambled on down to the mess hall, located in the basement floor of the building. Stopping at the small brown table just inside the mess hall door, I signed my name, rank, and serial number, picked up a tray and silver ware and got into the chow line. We were having steak today and I sure was ready to wrap my tongue around one of them. Patiently, I waited my turn as the line moved slowly forward until finally, I was standing in front of the civilian employee who was doling out the steaks. As I shoved my tray forward, this long-haired, greasy looking individual looked at me with a smile and said,

"Sorry, pal, we're all out of steaks. He got the last one." He said, pointing with his tongs at the guy in front of me.

I looked him up and down, then. He was taller than me by at least four inches, but he was thin. I probably outweighed him by twenty pounds. His blond hair hung straight and loosely to the bottom of his ear lobes and his nose, could have doubled as a birds beak, bell-bottomed jeans over dirty tennis shoes. I decided that I didn't like him.

I was disappointed, but I understood that if they were out, they were just out, and I would just have to settle for something else.

"Well, then," I said noticeably aggravated, "What HAVE you got?"

"Cold cuts," he answered with a slight curl to his lip that made the few scraggly hairs in his moustache stick straight out. I didn't care for his looks or his attitude.

"Cold cuts? You mean we go from steak to bologna, just like that?" I said, more agitated than ever.

"Just like that," he said, "take it or leave it, Pal."

I was getting hotter and hotter under the collar and the more we talked, the further south this conversation was going. I wasn't his "Pal" and I resented his calling me that. I decided that it would be in the best interest of us both if I just forgot about steaks and took my cold cuts from this sneering little draft dodger and sat down somewhere to cool down. I found a seat at a table opposite the guy who got the last steak. As luck would have it, as I sat fuming, the two guys who had been behind me in line came and sat beside me, they both had nice, big, juicy steaks on their trays.

Now, I was faced with a dilemma, should I just quietly sulk and eat the cold cuts in silence like this little hippy wannabe wanted me to do, or should I go back to the chow line and read him the riot act? I chose the latter. After all, I was a Sgt. in the US Army, not some wet behind the ears PFC that had only been in the service for a couple of months. I had been out of the country for a year and a half, I had paid my dues, and I refused to be treated this way. What right did this scurvy looking civilian have to withhold food from me anyway? The Mess hall was supposed to be first come, first served, and I had been there first. Picking up my tray, I went back to the steak man and reopened the dialogue.

"Just who in the hell do you think you are to give my food to someone who got in line behind me?" I asked. "Ain't you intelligent enough to know what first come, first served is?"

"I put those steaks back for my friends," he said angrily, "they told me that they were going to be late."

"That's not the way first come, first served works, you idiot," I said, giving vent to the little demon sitting on my shoulder. I then launched into a tirade denouncing him, his ancestors, his girlfriend, and the family dog...who I told him was probably also his girlfriend. Leaning a bit forward and sticking my chin out, I said, "I'm gonna have a steak, one way or the other." I was pushing, now secretly hoping, against hope, that he would open the ball, and to my amazement, he did, this greasy wad of fur leaned forward and open-handed, girl slapped me right on the left cheek. It was a decision that he instantly regretted. I had recently come here from a place where scuffles, great and small, were a daily occurrence and this sort of thing wasn't at all new to me. I wasn't a tough guy, I was just used to it. My right hand had balled up instinctively and was on its way to the point of his chin before I even knew. There was an audible "Thunk" as he was knocked backward and his legs began to stumble until he hit the wall behind him. He fell in a heap at the foot of that wall. He wasn't out, probably far from it, my punch had been long, I was reaching and it had lost a lot of steam on the way. Still, my "Pal," was done, and I had gotten my steak....one way or the other.

The next morning, Monday, there was a knock on my door. I opened the door to see the CQ runner. "Sgt. Suits," he said, "The CO wants to see you, ASAP." "Thanks, Durbin," I said, "I'll be right down."

Knocking on the CO's door, I heard a voice from inside that said. "Enter."

Coming to attention before the desk of Captain Dillard, the Commanding Officer of the 512th, I saluted saying, "Sir Sgt. Suits reporting as ordered."

"At ease Suits," he said, "I hear you were involved in a little fracas in the Mess Hall yesterday with Mess Sargent's son, I have already spoken with Staff Sgt. Bonner, now, I'd like to hear your side of this."

At the words, "The Mess Sargent's son." Caution lights began to flash in my mind. I had no idea, but I did know that this meant trouble for me. How could a prejudiced person, who wasn't even there, give a report that even approached accurately?

Knowing that Staff Sgt. Bonner hadn't even been in the building when our little spat happened, and hearing that Capt. Dillard had already gotten the story from him, assured me that regardless of anything I might say, I would be in the wrong. I was finding out, first hand that the old saying "The Army takes care of its own," was true. Bonner was a Staff Sgt., a lifer, I didn't have a prayer.

Standing at parade rest, I asked, "Do I even have a side, Sir?"

"Not really," he replied, "it's only a formality."

"What are my options, Sir?" I asked.

"Article 15, non-judicial punishment that'll cost you fifty bucks out of your next pay check, or, summary court-martial. If you lose there you could go to jail for a month. The choice is yours, Suits, you've got three days to make your decision. That is all."

Coming to attention once again, I saluted and said, "Thank you, Sir," did an about face, and left the CO's office.

I took that three days to think it over. I even went to the JAG (Judge Advocate General) office and spoke with a military lawyer. His advice was to take the Article 15. Fifty bucks wouldn't kill you and it wouldn't go on your record...it would be foolish to take this to a summary court martial and run the risk of jail time. I didn't take much time deciding to take the Article 15, but it certainly went against the grain. In my mind, I was justified, it was like telling Sargent

Bonner's little rat-faced boy that what he did was OK, but in my mind, it wasn't. Interestingly, I didn't see him in the Mess Hall anymore, maybe there was some justice, behind the scenes after all.

These events simply stoked the flames of my dislike for the 512th MP Company. Two weeks later, I was on the verge of asking for a transfer when the word came sown that they were asking for volunteers to work in the Stockade on post. I knew nothing about how a detention center worked, I only knew that it had to be better than being in the line company. I jumped at the chance to work somewhere else. I would be trained by, and be taking the place of, Sgt. Rudy Lopez, a Guard commander at the Ft. Huachuca Stockade. I had a couple of weeks, or so, of on-the-job training, and when Rudy left, I inherited the second squad, and had my own people again. Uniform of the day: helmet liner, web belt, and fatigues, brassard, and trousers bloused above shiny boots. It was almost like being back home. The personnel were great, completely different mind-set. The camaraderie and esprit de corps could be found in this little out of the way lock up. We were out in the hinterlands, we were left alone, we had our own hierarchy and Captain Dillard played a very small part in it. Volunteering for duty in the stockade at Ft. Huachuca Arizona, was the smartest thing I ever did.

While I was there, I was chosen as one of the body guards for the Honorable Stanley Reasor, then Secretary of The Army, on one of his infrequent visits to Huachuca. I was selected to join a very small number of handpicked MPs who made the trips to the state penitentiary at Yuma Arizona to transport prisoners back to Huachuca to face military charges. I was also presented with a "Letter of Commendation" by the Stockade commander, for outstanding performance of duty as Guard Commander and leader of the 2nd squad.

I served as a Guard Commander at that stockade until November 8th, 1972. In October, I was informed that I was getting out 60 days early. Before I left, though, I had the distinct privilege and honor of having one of the most outstanding individuals I have ever met, to not only join my squad of people and serve under me as a dedicated professional soldier but also who became my trusted lifelong friend and confidant, career soldier and First Sargent, William H. Hill Jr....but that's a whole 'nother story.

When I served at Ft. Huachuca, I was Twenty-two years old.

It was only yesterday.

My Daughter's Kite

The afternoon sun shining in long bright streaks, between the living room curtains, lit up the dust particles floating weightless in the air. I was in my easy chair, killing time on this Saturday afternoon, and also killing the last of a six-pack of Pabst Blue Ribbon. Shirtless, I brushed a fly from my shaved head as I took the last swallow. I wasn't drunk, at least not by my standards, just at that point where I was beginning to see the world a little differently than most folks. Suddenly, my daughter burst through the front door with a crash.

"Whoa," I said, wondering what was going on. "What's the matter? That's no way to come into a room."

"Daddy, that boy down the street stole my kite!" She said, shaking with anger and almost in tears, "And I want it back."

"What boy? what kite?" I managed, trying to focus on this new problem.

"That big boy about a half a block down on the other side of the street. I got it caught in a tree and he went up and got it loose but wouldn't give it back to me. He said I lost it and now it was his."

"He did, huh?" I said, conjuring up images of this young ogre stealing all the toys in the neighborhood. "Well, we'll just see about that. He might steal toys from other kids, but he's not gonna steal my daughter's kite."

I quickly put on my shoes and decided that I would just go up there and whip his dad to a frazzle for bringing such an inconsiderate little miscreant into the world. Nosiree, he would not have my daughter's kite, not today or any other day.

Still shirtless, I stepped out the door and began my march into combat. Head to toe, I was ready. Leaning slightly forward, my eyebrows formed one straight line over eyes that now peered from small slits. My lips were set and straight over a chin that jutted out slightly. The fingers of my large, strong hands were now clenched into large, white-knuckled fists as I waddled up the middle of

Standish Avenue to the showdown. Each step swelled my chest just a little more and fed a growing rage within me. This kid's dad was in trouble and he didn't even know it. He would know it soon, though, because I was coming for him, and I wouldn't be denied. At that moment, it wouldn't have mattered if his dad was Mohammad Ali, he had a butt-kicking coming and I was gonna give it to him. Maybe, after this, he'd teach his little criminal son to stop terrorizing the neighborhood. As my rage grew, so did my confidence, I was tough as a Hickory switch and today, I was gonna kick the crap out of his dad and prove to this little gangster-in-training that he couldn't steal anything from one of mine. As I approached his house, I could see the little unrepentant thief sitting on his front stoop and holding my baby's kite. Turning onto the front sidewalk and advancing quickly toward the house I shouted, in my fiercest tone,

"Boy, where IS your daddy?" In that instant, I thought of myself as a cross between a crocodile and a red-hot snapping turtle, and I could have taken his dad and six more just like him.

His answer, however, stopped this crocodile man in his tracks. He said, "I don't have one."

Instantly, and rightfully, my grossly oversized ego was deflated. It was as if he had struck a giant pin in my large balloon. All the confidence, all the anger, evaporated into thin air, and in their place were the all too familiar feelings of another nine-year-old boy, seventeen years earlier, who stood beside his mother as they came and told her that his daddy, too, was gone.

Instantly, I understood so many things about this boy. I understood his attitude, his need for attention, his unheard cry for help, but mostly, I understood his loss.

With a little questioning, I learned that he lived here with his grandmother and like his father, his mother was also gone. I had gone from "The Raging Bull," to the meekest of lambs. I had been put in my place by four words from a child, "I don't have one."

I gave the kid the kite and a promise to bring him a new ball of string....and my walk back down Standish Avenue wasn't the same as the walk up, it was much slower, and it was a different man who came back.

I was twenty-six.......

Buck's Haint

It was winter in Indianapolis. The temperature was somewhere down around the Brass Monkey stage and the snow was falling in great white wads, we already had eight inches with more to come. The wind was bawling like the North Pole Express, making it almost impossible to be outside without several layers of warm clothing. Stepping out into this winter wonderland, I instantly regretted it. I had to change the transmission in my old work van but I saw immediately that today wasn't going to be the day. Trying to jack up a van and change out the transmission in this snow, wind, and cold just wasn't something that was going to happen today. I needed a place in out of this weather...and I just happened to know someone who had one.

At the time, I lived in a small rental house right across the street from my landlord, my uncle Anuel Suits. Now, Uncle Anuel had a garage. It had been built behind his house, some years earlier. It was a block building, a two-car affair, with a loft where he would store Christmas decorations and such. One side had a grease pit built into the floor. The stairway to the loft was located against the wall right in front of the entrance to the grease pit. The grease pit was exactly what I needed. It would allow me to stand up under my van and work on the transmission, but most of all, it would allow me to do it inside, out of the cold, wind, and snow. I asked and got Uncle Anuel's consent to use his garage and I was all set. I towed my van over to his garage and with some difficulty, got it pushed in, by hand, and over the grease pit. After getting the van inside, I decided that I would start on it, first thing in the morning.

That evening, Donna and I were up at Aunt Mary and Uncle Anuel's house for supper when Buck (Uncle Anuel's nickname) began to tell me about the Haint that stayed in the garage.

"He doesn't mean any harm," Buck was saying, "sometimes, I can feel him touching my hair or blowing on the back of my neck. I just tell him to stop it, or that I'm busy and to leave me alone, and he does."

"You have got to be kidding me," I said, "if you've got a Haint, where did he come from....and what's he doing here."

"I have no idea where he came from and, as far as I can tell, he just hangs around, doing nothing but playing pranks on me."

"If I believed in that kind of stuff, I'd be just a little bit disturbed," I said with a certain amount of humor in my voice. "But I'd have to experience that stuff for myself before I'd give it too much thought."

Buck just gave me one of those knowing smiles and said, "Of you hang around here much, you will."

Sometime during the night, the snow stopped, leaving about ten inches of the cold, wet stuff covering everything, but the mercury in the thermometer had dipped further down and that wind had picked up and was biting cold. Morning came and with it, grey skies and more of the same. I tugged on my work clothes and boots, had my morning coffee, lugged my tools up to Buck's garage, and opened the door. A cat came running out and I thought, "You don't know what you're coming out into, cat, but I'm not gonna stand here and hold the door open for you to run in and out, you're on your own," and I closed the door behind me, shutting him out. The garage wasn't heated, but being inside, out of that wind was almost like sitting in front of one of those old potbellied Warm Morning wood stoves, like when I was little. With my trusty Thermos bottle full of hot, black, coffee, I could tolerate this.

Setting my tools on the garage floor, I slid them to the edge of the pit so I could reach them from underneath, and I lit up a cigarette. Blowing a smoke ring, I watched it disappear as I thought about the job I had to do. Take one out, put one in, it shouldn't be too hard. Of course, the transmissions were a little bit on the heavy side, but they were of the manual variety, for a light-duty, six-cylinder, and relatively small. I was a younger man, then, and accustomed to the rigors of hanging and finishing drywall....it wouldn't be a snap, but I could do it. Taking another drag on that cigarette and dreading to get started, I rigged up a trouble light, went to the front of the pit, and climbed down the ladder. Once down in the pit, I was at the perfect working height. I set about finding the right tools and then began taking the drive shaft loose from the rear end. The drive shaft out, I tied up the little manual transmission, to support the weight, and then began taking out the bolts. I could hear the wind, outside, it was sure kicking up a ruckus. After a little while, I had the Tranny loose. Standing on a couple of boards to raise me up a little higher and putting the weight of it on my shoulder I lifted, and carefully slid the splines back and free of the engine. As I set the tranny on the garage floor, at the edge of the pit, I heard a "Crash" in the loft. "That damned cat," I thought, "He's turned over a bunch of Buck's Christmas Decorations. Oh well, that kind of stuff happens when you've got cats." It was about this time that I remembered that I had let the cat out when I had come in, a fact that caused me to wonder what had caused the noise upstairs in the loft. I didn't think much about it though, as I had a lot of work still to do. Busying myself with the work in front of me, I wrestled the new transmission to the edge of the pit. Actually, it wasn't new, I had bought it from a junkyard with the guarantee that it would work.

"Crash!" Another round of things unknown, in the loft, falling, for reasons unknown. Now folks, I believe in the hereafter, and I believe that there is a realm that we just don't know too much about, it's spoken of in the book of Ephesians, Chapter 6, verse 12......but I don't believe in ghosts. Solomon said, in the book of Ecclesiastes, "The living know that they shall die, but the dead know not anything, neither have they any more a reward; for the memory of them is forgotten. Also, their love, their hatred, and their envy is now perished, neither have they any more a portion forever in anything that is done under the sun." So, people don't come back as ghosts. I still didn't think much about it. Then, I began to hear little noises, just random stuff, at first. A thump here, a long creeeeeeeak there. I set my work aside and just listened. I was starting to get just a little uneasy. The small noises above soon became a pattern, and then soon after that, the pattern became the distinct sound of footsteps on the board floor above. It wasn't just the hair on the back of my neck that was paying attention to the walker above, but my whole scalp was tingling. The footfalls above me were very distinct, they sounded like an old man in a nursing home as he shuffles to the end of the hallway and then turns around and shuffles back. Over and over, the footsteps went from one side of the loft to the other and then back again. By now, I was looking for some way to get out from under my van and out of that pit without having to climb up that ladder that was right under the black hole in the ceiling that was the entrance to the loft. Summoning all the courage I could muster, without looking up, I climbed up out of that pit, left my thermos bottle and all of my tools where they were, I left that little old man to stroll as long as he wanted to, and took myself to the warmth of my own living room.

No, I didn't imagine things, and no, I didn't let my imagination run away with me. I was a grown man, acquainted with the world, and not given to superstition or exaggeration. I know what I heard, and what I heard wasn't within the realm of the normal. I was starting to wonder about what Buck had told me. Later that evening, after Buck had gotten home from work, and saw that I was only half through with my Van, he said,

"I allowed that you'd be about finished up by the time I got home, what happened?"

I related to him the events of the day. He sat, listening, with that big, annoying grin on his face, I didn't think it was a bit funny.

"Well, son, you've just met the Haint," he said with that same knowing smile, "He doesn't mean any harm, he's just......around."

"Well," says I, "he can just be around. I don't want to be his friend, I don't want to be his buddy, I don't want to play his little games, I don't like anything about him. All I want is to get my van fixed and get it out of there."

By now, Buck was chuckling pretty hard, the next stage would be outright laughter. "Come on back up in the morning, Son," he said, between cackles, "it's Saturday, I'll help you get finished up."

"You've got yourself a deal," I said, relieved, "hopefully we won't have another visit from your little friend."

"If we do, I'll just tell him to go away," he said, still grinning.

This was my first and only encounter with Buck's Haint, a fact for which I am truly grateful. There have been other times in my life when I have experienced things of a similar nature, things that I can't use logic to explain away. I try to leave these things alone. There is one thing that's certain, though, no one's gonna tell me that there's not another realm, dimension, or some other place that is inhabited by beings that we don't know a whole lot about....and, now, forty-six years after the fact, I'm still a firm believer that Buck had a Haint.

I was twenty-seven.......

The Atomic Bomb

Several years ago, when I was a little younger, I ran across an ad in a Guns and Ammo magazine where the Lee Loading Company was offering a bullet mold for a 500-grain .45 caliber bullet. I had a little single-shot H&R .45-70, so I quickly decided that I needed that mold. Order it, I did, and when that red, black, and white box came in, I just couldn't wait to haul out the old melting pot and start pouring hot lead into that new mold. (A 500-grain slug, pushed fast enough, will knock an elephant down, and I just had to have some of THEM.) I cast about 50 of those slugs, ran them through the sizer-lubricator, and pressed on the gas checks. It was time to go to the books and find the right load. See, I didn't want something that would "Reach out and touch someone," I wanted something that would "Reach out and knock the pure-dee-crap out of someone." What I found wasn't just a strong load, it was actually diabolical. In essence, what I did was, turn my little H&R into something that killed at both ends when the trigger was pulled.

I only loaded a few at first because I wanted to get out and try them out. I grabbed my rifle and a fist full of shells and headed for the first place where I could set up a tin can, and start the lead flying downrange. It only took one shot for me to realize two things,

1. That I didn't want to pull the trigger again, unless I just had to, and

2. That I would have a lot of fun with this load as long as someone else was pulling the trigger.

I soon convinced my brother, James, to go out to the shooting range at Carrier Mills with me. We shot some mild factory loads for my little rifle, a few pistol and shotgun slugs....and then I hauled out five of those Atomic Bombs that I had made from old wheel weights.

"Here, try these out," I said, not giving any hint of what he was in for.

"How are they loaded?" he asked.

"They're pretty hot," I lied. (They were EXTREMELY HOT.) "I've already shot some of them, I just wanted to see what kind of group you can get with them."

With that, James settled in at the shooting table and loaded up. The hammer of my little H&R locked into the business position with that metallic that is so familiar to those who shoot. He drew a bead on the little paper target 50 yards downrange, and then, the silence was deafening....I waited for the blast. Seconds ticked by....3, 4, 5, I was watching James intently. This was gonna be good....6, 7, the trigger finger tightened almost imperceptibly, WHAM!!!!

The silence was broken with a deafening roar as that big slug started moving down the rifle barrel. As the smoke and fire belched out of that muzzle, 500-grains of pure-dee-hell fire streaked for the target.

Meanwhile, at the other end of the rifle, my brother's face twisted into a very slight grimace, as the butt of the rifle tried to tear through his shoulder muscles and break every bone within ten inches of it.

The muzzle jumped about a foot, the butt pushed back enough to move his shoulder, and as quickly as it had happened, it was over. I think that he was almost in shock. He rolled his head on that thick neck of his and just kinda stared at me, blankly.

"Well?" says I, trying hard to act as though I did this stuff every day. "What do you think?"

"Got anymore?" he asked, to my amazement.

I handed him another, WHAM!!!

Again, hell fire streaked for the target. The muzzle jumped high and I could almost feel the awful, bone-crunching recoil of that rifle butt. This scenario played out three more times. Finally, I said,

"I'm out of shells."

He paused and said, "THANK GOD. Those things ain't no good for nothin' but throwing away." Rubbing his shoulder he said, "This damned rifle kills at both ends." With that, he pulled back the sleeve of his T-shirt, and there it was proof that my brother was after all, human, like almost everyone else. The blood was rising to a point just under the skin, and the bruise was starting to show clearly. I guess I should have shown him my bruise, but, that would have made me human, too. I couldn't have that, could I?

I was thirty-years old.

The Compliment

"Scuse me, boys," I said to no one in particular. The guys who had been leaning on the big, chest-type pop cooler had already started to make room for me. "I just need one of them RC's out of there." With a quick scan of the bottle tops, I located the RC. Sliding the bottle over to the right to clear the bars and pulling it up, and out, I turned to get a bag of peanuts. Giving my aunt, Amy Gosser, my money, I turned back to the two men at the cooler.

I knew both of these men very well. The man with the cowboy hat was about the same height as I was, wore a long-sleeved western shirt, dark-rimmed glasses, and sported a dark brown Goatee and moustache, his name was Bob. The other man was my cousin, Virgil.

It was a Saturday in August 1979, squirrel season, and I had come to Uncle Joe's house for the weekend. Virgil and I always hunted squirrels, morning and evening on the weekends. Right now, we were taking a mid-day break and I had just walked in on a conversation between the two other Vets. Pouring some of my peanuts into my RC, I stood there and listened.

"I sure as hell don't want to go back." I heard Virgil say with conviction. "I've spent all the time there I'm gonna spend. Thirteen months is plenty long enough to get shot at. If they was to want me to go again, they'll have to find me."

"Me neither," Bob said, "I've seen the last of Viet Nam. If they ever call me to go back again, I'm going straight to the deep woods of Canada."

Munching on the cola-soaked peanuts and taking a pull on the RC, I was awed at Virgil's next statement. "Not me," he said, "Mike is an MP and he knows as much about the woods as I do."

It was then that I realized that Virgil had a very deep respect for my abilities as a woodsman. I had never thought much about it but Virgil had let me know, with that simple statement, that he believed that I was a woodsman on a par with himself, a compliment of the highest order coming from someone of Virgil's caliber. It meant that Virgil, unknown to me, had watched me, many times when we were afield. He had seen, first hand, how I handled and reacted to things that came up while we were in the woods. It meant that he had watched and listened to me as I spoke about what I thought our quarry was going to do after we had been winded.

As I poured another round of peanuts into the neck of my RC bottle, my mind went back to one such occasion on a cold day the previous winter. Virgil and I had taken a hike out behind the store. There was an eight-inch blanket of snow on the hills and hollers between the store and Saline Creek. The snow had come during the night and we were the first to wade into the pristine whiteness and destroy that smooth, white surface. Virgil had carried his trusty old twelve gauges and I had opted for my .30/06 with a twenty-power Tasco sitting on top. That rifle weighed fourteen lbs.

Passing by the fingers that opened into the gully where the little stream flowed, unfrozen by the harsh temperature, we came to the edge of the large meadow. Up ahead, about six hundred yards, we could see four deer that had been spooked by our coming down the gully, running at full tilt.

"Well, shoot," Virgil said, "we might have got one of them if we'd have been a little more careful."

"We still might," I said. "If they do what I think they'll do, we can get up ahead of them and they'll come right over top of us. I think they're gonna make a big circle and come right back behind us. All we've gotta do is get up on top of that ridge and wait, they'll come right to us, but we'll have to hurry."

"Ain't no way," Virgil said, "those guys are headed out of the country, they've already winded us."

"Tell you what," I said, "you follow their tracks and I'll head for the ridge up there. I expect that in about thirty minutes we'll be seeing each other again."

"Bull crap," he had said, with a smile, "in about thirty minutes I'll have to fire off a couple of rounds to let you know where I am."

"Dreamer," I said, hoping that I was right, "bet you a dollar."

"You're on," he said, "I can already feel my bill fold getting bigger."

Turning north, I stayed in the tree line as I trudged toward the distant ridge, the thick blanket of wet snow hampering my progress with every step. I could still see Virgil, halfway across the meadow, following the tracks of the deer.

Stopping to catch my breath, I shifted the heavy rifle to the other shoulder before continuing to climb to the top of the ridge. Gaining the top, I immediately began looking for the deer. Sadly, I had gotten there too late. Looking down, I could plainly see the tracks of four deer that had already passed by the place where I was standing and were now probably heading for parts unknown. I had been too slow.

Leaning against a large Oak tree, I waited for the tiny, distant figure that I knew was Virgil, to follow those tracks right on up the ridge to me.

"Well, I'll be damned," he said, "you were right about this one. Did you see them?"

"Nope," I returned, "they came through before I could get up here, walking in this damned snow is just too slow for me. Actually, we were both right," I continued, "I thought they'd double back, and they did.....you thought they'd leave the country, and they did. I guess the bet's off." We had spent the rest of the day walking all over those hills, from Saline Creek to the old farm and back to the same store where we were now.

Coming back to the present, and not really knowing what to say in answer to Virgil's comment, I blurted, "That's pretty high praise."

"Nooo, honey," he drawled, "that's not just idle praise, that there is the God's honest truth, if I ever told it. I'd be proud to have you with me in the woods, any time.

That long-ago compliment from Virgil, "He knows as much about the woods as I do," put me on par with men who were capable of going off into the woods with a gun and knife and surviving, men like Virgil.

It was High Praise, Indeed.

I was thirty-years old

Ducks

I never cared too awful much for duck – the meat, I mean. I always thought they were harder to clean than chickens and the meat was just too oily to suit my taste. I have always been a hunter, though, and so when the opportunity came to take my boat out across the fields and through the woods that were now covered with the very early spring's backwater and hunt some ducks, I was all too willing.

I was spending the weekend down at Uncle Joe's house, down on Suits Hill, in Hardin County, in the spring of 1980. We were sitting around the breakfast table just shootin' the breeze when Virgil said, "Why don't we take your boat over to Mud Lake and shoot some ducks?"

"What makes you think that there are ducks over there?" I replied, "and that's a pretty far piece."

"I reckon there's ducks a'plenty over there right now," he said, "besides, what with the backwater in, we could put in right there at Beaver Creek and just go straight through the woods, it wouldn't take no time." When breakfast was over, we donned our cammo, grabbed our shotguns, and headed out.

I had a twelve-foot, wide bottomed, aluminum Jon boat that I sometimes hauled in the back of my pick-up truck, mostly when I was going to Uncle Joe's house. I pushed it with a nine-and-a-half horsepower, short-shaft Johnson motor. That motor was perfect for the places that I took this boat. I did a lot of fishing on Saline Creek's small tributaries and many times the channels would be blocked by a log that might be sitting a few inches above the surface of the water. With this motor, I could get a run at the wet, slick offending log, let my speed carry the boat over the top, and just as the back of the boat reached the log, pull forward on the motor, raising the propeller out of the water, and in just seconds I would be on the other side of the log on my way, we called it "Skipping the logs."

The backwater was on "stand" right about now so there was no current to the water. The water was everywhere, though, even the highway across the Harris Creek Flats was under about four feet of it. Corn and bean fields now looked like they were part of one huge lake. This was one of those nasty, grey, days. The temperature wasn't freezing, but it was down in the uncomfortable zone. That, coupled with the mist in the air, should have made us want to just stay at home in the warm, But, nooooo, we needed to go over to Mud Lake and shoot us some ducks. Everything around us was still dressed in the colors of winter. Everything, it seemed, was either grey or some shade of it, light grey, dark grey, and everything in between, except for the backwater, it was muddy brown. In our cammo, and my boat, which was a grey-green color, we blended into things right well. (Something that would serve us very well in a couple of hours.) We put the boat in Beaver Creek. It was much easier today because, like all the other creeks in the area, including Saline Creek due to the backwater, it was out of its bank and we could launch from flat ground. Guiding the boat through the woods, I made just as straight a line for Mud Lake as I could. We came to a place where there were no trees for a long stretch.
"Saline Creek," I said to Virgil, "we can follow it for a couple of minutes."
He only nodded in reply, I turned the boat to the east, once again entering the woods, Mud Lake was only about 10 minutes away. Reaching the lake, I could see the surface was covered with ducks, and more flying in and out...this was gonna be a good day. Shutting off the motor, we sat for a few minutes, letting the noise of our arrival settle down into the quiet that was all around us. Uncasing our guns, we missed a couple of ducks.
"Dang," I began,
"Shhhh," Virgil said, holding up a palm and tilting his head. "Listen!"
From somewhere far away, I could just barely make out the sound of an outboard motor.
"Start her up and let's get out of here," he said.
"Why," I answered, puzzled. "We just got here."
"We're gonna have company shortly," he said, "my guess is that that will be the Game Warden docked at Saline landing. If you don't want to lose your boat and guns and pay a bunch of fines, you'd better start this rig up pronto and head for the house."

He didn't have to waste any time on further explanations because I had the motor running and was on the move. Now I didn't have any notions that my little twelve-foot Jon boat could outrun a government-sponsored Game Warden's boat so I would have to think this one through, but I'd have to do it on the move.

I figured that they would be headed for Mud Lake, and if they did, they'd have to go through some woods too. Since they were coming from Saline Landing, southwest of us, I knew that we could head off to the northwest and stay out of their sight, at least for a little bit. When they got to Mud Lake and found that we weren't there, they'd have to shut off their motor in order to hear us...but when they did, and they certainly would, the chase would begin in earnest. I weaved my little boat through the woods as fast as I could, trying to get to the other side of the channel of Saline Creek. That was hill country there and I knew my way around, even in the backwater. Skipping a few logs, I made it to that long stretch with no trees, and knowing that I was over Saline Creek kept right on going until we were swallowed up by the big timber beyond. About two hundred yards into the woods, I ran across a big wad of Honeysuckle. Pulling the boat to the backside of this I shut the motor off. Virgil and I both reached out and grabbing the Honeysuckle, pulled it up and over our boat and ourselves, we were completely covered, boat, motor, occupants, and all in the wet, dripping, thick vines of that Godsend of a plant. With the motor off, we could clearly hear them coming up the channel of Saline Creek. It was only a matter of minutes till we saw them. Their boat was much bigger than mine and had a much bigger motor hanging off the back, that thing was built for speed. Only our knowledge of the woods, the creek and where the bends were, and the terrain, kept us from being seen out in the open. We sat there, under our Honeysuckle hideout, for the better part of an hour while the Game Wardens ran back and forth, up and down the main channel of Saline Creek. We watched, in fascination, as they tried, in vain, with binoculars to locate us. They would go out of sight, and hearing, to the north and then, gradually, we would hear them coming back. We could see them again, trying to probe the deep woods with their glasses, all to no avail. I guess they didn't want to risk taking that larger boat, with its oversized motor, into the deep woods. Whatever the reason, after about an hour and a half, we heard their boat go out of sight, and hearing, to the South. We waited until we were sure that they were gone and then came out from under our tent and headed home. It was one of many good times and we laughed, the laughter of reckless youth. We had outwitted the powers that be. We had broken into their castle, stolen the goose that laid the golden egg and escaped with our lives and fortunes. We had no way of knowing that this was to be our last great adventure together. Next year, this same old dirty piece of water would take Virgil, and in doing so would end a way of life for me.

I was thirty-one......

The Death of Virgil

"Hey, Suits," someone yelled, over the din of shooters and onlookers at the Dale trap club. "Someone wants to talk to you." I placed my shotgun in the long, wooden rack beside forty or fifty others, and began to make my way to the clubhouse. Waiting for me outside the little, white, rectangular building, I found my niece.

She was a sharp contrast to all the other people around me. She was tall, with long, silky, dark hair blowing in the breeze. Her jacket wasn't heavy enough for the early April chill. Her folded arms told me that she was cold and impatient and that she really wanted to be someplace else. As I came closer, I noticed the tears in her eyes and the slight shiver in her shoulders. My heart began to race, something was wrong. I began to brace myself for the news that I was almost afraid to hear.

"What's wrong, Sis?" I asked.

"Uncle Joe wants you to come, right now," she said, "they think that Virgil has drowned."

Impossible, I reasoned within myself as I stood, motionless. Not Virgil, he was too smart, too savvy. Instinctively, I knew where this tragedy would have happened, had it been possible. Virgil and I had hunted and fished that old creek for years and we were both very well acquainted with all the aspects of the place.

We had camped there as kids, among the ancient hardwood trees. The tall, thick oaks stood like silent sentinels, guarding the secrets of days gone by. The green, oblong leaves of the stately Hickory Trees gave them the appearance of tall, bushy, grey lamp posts. All of nature, in that place, seemed to touch the very face of heaven. This place was special.

The creek that ran by, confined by high, slick banks, had been the source of many evening meals. It had also been the source of many ghost stories, told late at night. By day, the creek was a beautiful place to behold, blue-green water with dashes of green, red, yellow, and brown, pushing up from its edge. Sunlight glistened like a million tiny candle flames on the surface of the water. By night, it was an eerie place, especially for kids. The timber owls that had slept through the day, now inhabited the heights of those magnificent trees, and as if on some secret cue, had begun their chorus of night music. The strains of that music could be heard, now here, now there, but always close. That blue-green water, by now, had turned black and now resembled a long, black ribbon covered with a piece of smooth glass. By night, something, we were sure, lurked beneath that smooth ribbon of blackness.

"Where did it happen?" I rolled the words through disbelieving lips.

"Over on Saline Creek, where you guys always fish," she said. The tears that had been in her eyes now became a torrent, as fear and confusion gushed out of her. "Oh, Uncle Mike, 'Hurry,'" she said.

I quickly stowed my shooting gear and began the forty-mile trip to Hardin County. The oncoming headlights and road signs made little impression on me as I raced to be with my uncle. All thoughts of shooting little clay targets were gone, and my mind focused on Virgil.

Virgil, was my cousin, the only son of my father's brother. Dark, curly, almost kinky hair, combed back from a high, tanned forehead, gave him the appearance of a middle-aged Indian. Strong fingers that spoke of hard work from an early age, had skinned almost every kind of animal that the deep woods of Hardin County had produced. Not an overly large man, he had a medium-heavy build. He was a kind, gentle man, who never spoke ill of anyone without just cause. A combat veteran of the Jungles of Vietnam, he was soft-spoken, never bragged about his exploits, and showed all men that most basic of courtesies, respect. Virgil was more than my cousin, he was my best friend.

I crossed Beaver Creek and began the ascent up the steep hill that lies just on the border of Gallatin and Hardin Counties. A mile further down the road, I pulled my car into Uncle Joe's already crowded driveway. As I opened the door of that dear old man's home, I was met with the blank stares of family and friends.

Crossing the living room, quickly, I entered the kitchen of the house that my grandfather had built, many years ago. My eyes took in the small white desk to the left of the doorway. To the right, the small sewing table that had belonged to my grandmother now held the telephone. The white enameled cabinets, the stove, the paper towel holder, these things that were so familiar to me, now, seemed to be only useless things, as I searched for the face that I knew would tell me if the story was true.

Sitting at the end of the large brown table, was the dear old man who had played such an important role in my childhood. The years had taken his robust frame, along with some of his hair. Where there had, years ago, been thick, dark hair, there was now only a wisp, to comb straight back. Dark-rimmed glasses ringed those red, moist eyes that were so full of pain. The square jaw was fighting desperately to hold back the wave of grief that was mounting just behind his quivering lips. One scarred, old hand rested on the table, the other hung loosely at his side. In spite of all the pain, there was a quiet dignity about the man. I loved Virgil, but I loved this old man more.

My searching look asked the question, and in reply, he simply said, "Son, I think he's gone. He came up once and hollered, and then, I didn't see him anymore." It was then that I realized that Uncle Joe had seen it happen in the half-light of dusk. They had been coming upstream in a little ten-foot Jon boat, three men a tubs of fishing gear. The rain had caused them to wear heavy rubber boots and rainsuits. It was taken for granted that all the men could swim so the life jackets were left on the bank in order to make more room for fishing gear. The boat was heavily loaded. With such a burden, the little boat sat only inches out of the water. As the little boat struggled to push its cargo against the current, water began to rush in over the front. As Virgil yelled, "We're taking water," the man in the middle of the boat stood up. The motion of the slowing boat made him lose his balance and he plunged forward, over the front of the boat, taking Virgil into the black water with him. As I listened to the ghastly account, I realized that I must go to that eerie place, and if I couldn't help, then I would simply be there. Virgil, must not be alone.

The scene that met me, as I drove down the winding little lane to the creek, was one that I never expected. There were rows of lights, vehicles, and people, so many people. Some handled lights, some radios, and some just hung around and watched the commotion. As I looked around, I noticed that our little portion of the creek was lit up, almost to the point of daylight, but still, that black ribbon gave no hint of what lay beneath the surface.

As dawn came, my sleepless eyes began to catch glimpses of an overturned boat, a wash tub that once held the long gill nets, the casually discarded life jackets. The people were coming back now, anticipating the arrival of the divers. At this moment, I hated them, these people who came only to see the spectacle. It seemed, somehow, irreverent. This was, for the moment, a resting place for the dead and should be approached with reverence.

From my vantage point, the divers looked like so many hump-backed men, bobbing up and down in the water. At about 11:00 a.m. one of the divers called for a basket, they had found one of the bodies.

All hope, now gone, I made my way to the steep bank and reached down to pull the loaded basket from the water. As I pulled with the other three or four men, I looked down into the still face of my cousin. Eyes slightly open, eyebrows raised, I could see that he had struggled to reach the life-giving air. I saw no fear in the face of this man, only resignation. He knew, that the reaper had come for him, that death was upon him, and he faced death as he had faced life, bravely changing the things that he could change, and just as bravely, accepting the things that he knew to be inevitable.

I don't go there anymore. That special place from my childhood now holds memories that spoil my enthusiasm. I have come to know that life hangs by a very fragile thread and that one small mistake in judgement can mean the end of it. Age and experience should not make one lose respect for the things around him. If anything, they should bring more caution. We both knew what that old creek was capable of, but, somehow, over the years, we had forgotten that we were not immortal. Virgil, like me, had lost respect for the creek. That one small error in judgement took the life of my cousin and friend and caused me to respect the creek once more.

If a man loses respect for something that, under the right circumstances, can be a deadly enemy, he puts himself at risk.

As for that old black ribbon, well, it just flows on as if nothing happened......

I was thirty-three

The Solution

Back in about June of 1989, I heard from someone that there was to be a boat race on the Ohio River, from Cave-In-Rock to Golconda Illinois, a distance of about twenty-five miles. It was all part of a yearly celebration at Cave-In-Rick called (I think) Frontier Days. The race was called 'The Davey Crockett River Race.' At the time, there were only two contestants in the race, Hardin County and Pope County. Now I, being an old Hardin County boy, quickly decided that if it was possible, I'd be on that Hardin County boat, defending the honor of the county from which I and my people had sprung. Race day came, warm and humid and with much fanfare....and I, through some conversations with folks that I knew, got the "Go Ahead," and would be manning an oar on the "Hardin County Belle."

In the tiny little river town of Cave-In-Rock, there was a carnival atmosphere. There was food, of all kinds. There were rides and games, even a Rendezvous, where folks dressed in period clothing, had shooting contests with black powder rifles, had Tomahawk throwing contests, and camped in Tepees while cooking their meals on an open fire....in Hardin County, it was a Big Deal. In addition to all the locals, there were people from miles and miles away, from counties North and West, even folks from across the river in Kentucky, who all gathered to witness and take part in, the festivities.

It was my honor and distinct pleasure to be among those men who manned the oars of the "Belle". There is a certain camaraderie that develops between men who share a common task, goal, or hardship, it was not a job for the faint of heart.

When I first climbed into the "Belle," I noticed that there were no seats. To compound that error, on the inside of the boat, the oars were tied together with a length of conduit. This was done in an effort to keep the oars synchronized. It was a good idea, in theory, but it was flawed. What if you broke an oar? You would be dead in the water until the oar was repaired. Tying the oars together would also allow a tired man, or a shirker, to ease off of his oar, thus forcing the other oarsmen to take up the slack. The result would be that the other oarsmen would tire much more quickly and the overall speed of the boat would suffer. At this time, Hardin County hadn't won a race yet and this day would be no different.

From the starting gun, we watched, in anger, as the "Lady Lusk" pulled ahead of us and got smaller and smaller as the distance separating us got larger and larger. We went down in defeat, Pope County had won again. Not accustomed to losing, indignantly, I made up my mind, right then and there, that next year, I would build a boat, get a crew, and introduce the crew of "Lady Lusk" to the Losers Circle.

I got started immediately. I contacted Ray Harris, the gentleman who was in charge of the race and got specifications for the boat that I would build. There was a certain design for the boats involved that had to be followed so that everything was equal, even down to the weight. The boats could be no more than sixteen feet long, eight feet wide, and eight feet high. Each boat had to have six oars and a tiller that was mounted on the top, and to the rear of the boat, oars had a maximum length of thirteen feet, seats were optional. I had a friend, Butch Reece, who wanted to be a part of this enterprise, so I let him be the fundraiser. Butch was well-liked in the community and had a line of bullshit a mile long, he was a natural salesman. It wasn't long before the donations began to come in.

I had sat for hours and hours designing the boat. I drew up a blueprint and went over every item, piece by piece. I would put this boat together with bolts and screws. I would use adhesive, where I could, this boat must not leak. This boat would have seats. The oarsmen would, at least, have some semblance of comfort as they pulled on those oars and turned the palms of their hands into hamburgers. There would be individual oar locks so that any oar could be inserted or removed in seconds. The stems of the oars were built from Ash wood. I had them cut two inches square and twelve feet long. The blades were made of Pine, and shaped after the fashion of modern oars. I tapered all the edges of the blades so that they could be easily dipped into and out of the water. I cut long slots into the ends of the oar stems. I rounded the last two feet of the wood so that the oarsmen would have a comfortable grip on the oar. The oars were finished with two coats of Spar Urethane. Finally, I added the oar locks. There was a boat manufacturer in Eldorado, at the time, and in lieu of a donation, they offered to coat the bottom eighteen inches or so, of the hull, inside and out with fiberglass and outside, that fiberglass would be covered with gel coat. This procedure would guarantee that the hull would not leak, it was an offer that I was more than happy to accept. When the roof was finally finished, I coated it also with Spar Urethane, and into this wet Urethane, I sprinkled good amounts of sand to form a non-skid surface for the tillerman to walk on.

I must say, at this juncture, that my buddy Butch liked to tell folks that "We" built this boat...and I guess in one sense "We" did. Butch did get the biggest part of the donations that allowed me to purchase the material to build the thing, but make no mistake, it was me who put it all together, on my own. My fingerprints were on every single bolt, screw, piece of wood, or tube of glue that went into the building of this boat. My old buddy would come out and babysit his kids while sitting in the shade of the big Walnut tree in my backyard, and, beer in hand, happily watch as I sweated my ass off putting things together. I didn't really mind this though because I wanted it built the way "I wanted it built." I had experience with wood and building procedures, but he did not. After all, there would be more than thirty men who would rely on my ability to build a boat that would stay in one piece and bring them safely back to shore at race's end, and I fully intended for that to happen.

Finally, the boat was finished. I painted the upper part of the hull brown and the lower, gel-coated part, was white. With the help of my neighbor, David Dudley, we hauled the boat to his pond for a trial run. She handled it beautifully, I couldn't have been happier. There were only three things that remained to be done. I had to name the boat, I had to get a crew and support boat, and lastly, I had to win that race.

Naming the boat proved to be more difficult than one might expect. I wanted something that would reflect where we were from, Saline County. There would be four entries this year, Hardin County, Pope County, The Job Corp, and us, Saline County. I didn't want some hokey, funny name that people would laugh at, I wanted something that stood out. There were many suggestions, The Old Salt, The Old Tar, and many other such names ranging from some that were good, all the way down to quite stupid sounding. Once again, my old buddy, Butch, came in with a winner, and we named it the "Saline Solution." Plater's printing shop had said that they would make up the Vinyl, and stick on letters, for both sides of the boat when we decided on a name, so the name problem was solved.

Next came the problem of getting enough men together to row a three-thousand-pound boat twenty-five miles down the sometimes-rough waters of the Ohio River with its wind and barge wakes. The call was put out and surprisingly, we had more than enough sons of Saline County who were more than eager to volunteer for a seat on the "Solution." This was not only an adventure, but we saw it as the premier sporting event in the whole country. We had more than enough men to make up five six-man crews and two tiller men. A gentleman named Gary Martin volunteered to bring his pontoon boat as our support boat. It would carry all the crew members who were not rowing and would stay close behind the Solution so that when it was time to change crews, we could do so very quickly, problem number two, was solved.

We didn't really think that problem number three, winning the race, was actually a problem. See, back then, we were younger and we were well endowed with courage and confidence. No task was too hard and no challenge was too great to go unanswered,

we had the will to win.

Race day, in June of 1990 came with the same heat and humidity as its predecessor, with the same fanfare and excitement. The water was anything but calm. The barges, with their giant wakes, and the motor boat and jet-ski traffic conspired with the wind to make sure that this day's work would not be an easy one. The boats had been weighed at the truck scales at the rock quarry and all were within a few pounds of each other, except us....they said that we were about two hundred pounds lighter than the other entries so they made us carry two hundred pounds of tractor weights in our boat.

The starting crew on the Solution was made up of four of the five Suits brothers, and two nephews, all family and all stout construction men, what a team that was. My old uncle, Orlando Suits (we called him Uncle Arlen) had come down to the river, before we lined up for the start, to inspect my boat. After looking it over from stem to stern, he could find nothing that he would have done differently....and if you knew my old Uncle Arlen, you'd know that, that alone was High Praise.

We rowed the Solution out into the third position in the deep choppy water of the Ohio and waited for the gun. Everyone had a stomach full of butterflies, the air was filled with excitement. The anticipation was almost a living thing.

"Come on, come on," Gary muttered.

"Fire the gun!" somebody else echoed, "let's get started!"

Our oars were just under the surface of the water, waiting, for that tremendous, sudden pressure that would be required to move that ton and a half of wood, fiberglass, and steel against the wind and waves.

"BANG!" The starting gun sounded. The cheers went up from the spectators who were lined up and down the banks of the river. As one, we strained against the muddy green water. Arms and legs quivered and the Solution responded and moved forward. The butterflies were gone, instantly, as we pulled the oars with all we had. The boys on the Lady Lusk had gone through many practice sessions on this river, and more than one race. They were good, I had to admit, and they put on quite a show as they pulled out in front at the outset. But we were not there for any show, we had come to take the trophy home to Saline County. When she got fifty yards ahead, I gave the word to my crew, "OK, boys, let's catch 'em"! Together, we leaned into the oars and caught them in just a little while. It was hard going, we were tired, blisters were forming in the palms of our already calloused hands, still, we pressed on. They were rowing furiously in an effort to keep us at bay, but to no avail. We caught up to them and, too late, they realized what we were doing. Our plan was to change crews as soon as we came abreast of the Lady Lusk. It worked perfectly. Our support boat, the large pontoon boat, pulled up to our rear and while other crew members held it tightly against the Solution by means of two ropes, one on either side, that were affixed to the Solution, my crew left the boat, going through the right side of the large, square opening in the back while a new crew came onboard from our left. The change was over in eleven seconds. We had a fresh crew that was just aching to do battle with the Lady Lusk, and they hadn't even called up their support boat. Their crew was exhausted and we had "New Meat" behind our oars. Before they could get changed out, we were a hundred yards ahead, a lead that we would broaden, until we broke an oar.

We pulled in to the bank at Elizabethtown for a scheduled fifteen-minute break. As we touched the bank, our time was noted as were the other boats. The Lady Lusk came in five minutes behind us, which meant that she couldn't leave

E-town until five minutes after we left. The next stop was Rosiclare where we took half an hour to eat lunch. Same drill, we were timed, in and out. A race judge released us and we were off, as fast as our crew could row.

Somewhere on the river, a couple of miles after we left Rosiclare, one of our guys broke an oar. This was a problem of Biblical proportions. The problem was that I had neglected to make any extras, we had six and only six. We were crippled by the loss of the oar and the sixteen and one half percent of our rowing power. This catastrophe was witnessed by many jet-ski riders and ski-boat drivers and soon the word was spread as far back upriver as Cave-In-Rock. Soon, everyone on the river, between Cave-In-Rock and Golconda, knew that the Saline Solution had broken an oar and was in danger of losing the race. Pope County was elated and when they changed out crews they let their support boat, a very long and very wide river jon, with a many horse-powered motor, push them for as long as it took for them to change out their crews, and they took their time. There was no doubt that we were in trouble. The Lady Lusk was gaining on us. It was obvious that if things continued at the present rate, we just might lose, a prospect that didn't set well with any of our crews. We continued the fight and just when it seemed that all was lost, for the Lady Lusk was right behind us, a ski-boat appeared, between us and the bank of the river. The driver pulled up close beside us and said,

"The 'Belle,' has dropped out of the race, along with the Job Corp boat. We heard that you boys had met with a little mishap, and so, since we've dropped out, we want you boys to have these." With that, his passenger began passing two of the Belle's oars over to our grateful arms. "Our only request is that you beat those sons-a-bitches from Pope."

Elated, I said, "Consider it done, and thank you." Slamming the gift from the guys of Hardin County, into our oar lock, once again, I said, "Thank You," as we dug into the waves with a renewed purpose.

Looking over the water, abreast of us, I could see the panic, the frustration in the eyes of the exhausted oarsmen on the Lady Lusk. They had seen the oar delivery and they knew what it meant. It would pump new life into our crews. It would restore our belief that we would win. It would mean that we were no longer crippled. It meant that we were back in the race, and, for us, it meant that they would lose.

With renewed confidence and strength, we pulled on the oars slowly regaining our lead. Blistered hands, sun-burned faces, and aching backs forgotten, we rowed feverishly to increase that lead, for it seemed that every time our lead was comfortable, they would change crews and gain on us significantly. Finally, the Golconda Marina came into sight and this was where the race got serious. The crews on both boats were determined that their boat would be the first to cross the finish line. Apparently, we were more determined of the two crews for we crossed about twenty feet ahead of the Lady Lusk. The Saline Solution's maiden voyage had been successful, she had won her first race. She won three of the four races she was entered in. She was crewed by dedicated individuals who possessed a drive, a will to win, and I will be forever grateful to these sons of Saline County for their sweat, for their blood, for their aches and pains, but mostly because they were willing. It is true that every man who pulled an oar or tiller, on the Saline Solution, and every person who supported our endeavor, whether it was money, food, supplies, or time, is owed a debt of gratitude for helping to make The Saline Solution the winner that she was.

She brought me much joy!

I was forty years old.....

Grits

I love grits. I puts sweetnin' down in there, an' a little wad of butter, but they's fine, with or without.

When my wife got out of the hospital an' came home, she had one of them foller up Dr. Appointments. So, we went over West of our town to keep it. After her appointment, we decided to stop in at one of them popular eatin' joints an' have us a nice big breakfast. My, my, we ordered up one of them super, dyna whoppin' big un's! What come with bacon, sausage, biscuits an' gravy, lots of them aigs an' fried taters; a big ol' dish of them fried apples, lots of butter an' jelly....an' Grits. We was a havin' such a fine time. We was a laughin'an' a gigglin', an' all while, forkin' that grub down. Now, I got almost done a cleanin' up my plate when I decided that right now would be a good time to treat myself to them grits. I puts just the right amount of sweetnin' in there, an' that little wad of butter, (Which I let melt as I carefully stirred that butter an' sweetnin' together) an' then began to spoonin' them grits sown. Lawdy, them grits was some kind of somethin' or another. I got down to my last spoonful an' noticed, there, down in the bottom of the dish, was three little small black things. Now, me, bein' curious by nature. I takes the spoon an' dips up one of them little black spots an' calls our waiter feller over to our table.

"Reckon you could tell me what this here is?" I says to him.

"Looks like burnt rice to me," he replies.

"Well," says I, "they do kinda resemble burnt rice, but I reckon I know a mouse turd when I see one."

Instantly this feller launches into a defense of his kitchen that would have made Stormin' Norman proud.

"Hold on there, Partner," says I, "I'm not tryin' to get a free meal here, I'll pay for what we got...an' it won't affect your tip none, unless you're the guy what shit in my grits, just don't try to tell me it's burnt rice. I've been around long enough to know what mouse turds is."

He gives me one of them, "I hate you," looks an'says, "I'll show it to my manager."

Off he goes, a holdin' a mouse turd decorated spoon up over his head. Presently, he comes back to our table, minus the spoon an' wearin' a crestfallen expression on that face.

"My manager says it's a mouse turd." He mumbles, not a thank you, screw you, "Sorry, or how can we make this right, nothing."

Now, I told you all this little story for two reasons. One was because I thought you all might get a laugh out of it, and two, to remind you to always look your food over if you didn't cook it yourself. Just because an eatin' joint is pretty popular, that doesn't mean that you won't run across a mouse turd every now an' then.

I was 72 years old

Grits II

Only a few days ago, Donna and I were in Marion again, seems like when you get to be a senior citizen, you also get to visit a doctor's office much more frequently than you used to. My appointment was early this time, so by 8:30 a.m. I was finished and outta there. Donna had remarked that she could stand a little something to eat, and my stomach, always ready for the next challenge, agreed. We decided, after a year and a half of boycott, to give that popular eating joint another chance at serving up a nice bowl of grits for breakfast. After all, lightning never strikes twice in the same place, does it?

Well sir, we strolled on over to that old Coca Cola Cooler that they have a settin' half in the doorway to the dinin' room, an' waited for that nice waitress lady to show us where it was that she wanted us to sit. We parked ourselves at a table right up next to the window and began to look over the menu. Immediately, we noticed that the menu had changed somewhat from the last time we were there. The prices for the different breakfasts had pretty much stayed the same, but now, the breakfasts came with fewer and fewer side dishes. For instance, those grits that I wanted to have with my breakfast, didn't come with it anymore! They were two dollars extra, now. Same with the fried apples and a few other things. Now, I being a nice, calm individual who isn't given to sarcasm, accepted this unwelcome change as just part of the continuing saga of "How to Gouge Your Fellow Man." I didn't like it, but under the circumstances, I was powerless to do anything about it. Scowling at the menu from under wrinkled eyebrows I said, "Looks like if we're gonna have grits this morning, it's gonna cost us four dollars more than it used to, heaven forbid that we'd want fried apples and a little dish of gravy too! Good grief, can you believe that they want two dollars for a little bowl of grits?"

"Now, honey," Donna replied, in her sweet way, "everything's higher now than it was before, that's just the way it is."

"That may be the way it is," I replied, rather testily, "but why? Does it suddenly cost more to make grits now? Is it supply and demand –more people suddenly eating grits now?" And then, answering my own question, I said, "No! It's just plain greed."

Putting an end to tirade, she answered sweetly, "Well, greed or not, honey, if you eat grits this morning, you're gonna give two dollars for them." She was right, of course, so rather than try to continue an argument that I had already lost, I contented myself with scowling at the menu and complaining about the slow service.

The waiter finally came to our table, armed with a pen and order book, a name tag that said "Eugene" and a look on his face that said, "It doesn't matter what you order I'm gonna get it wrong." We ordered our breakfast, being careful to include the expensive grits, and watched as Eugene swished away with our order. While we waited, my mind travelled back to the last time I had eaten grits in this place. I had been in this very room and as I recalled, I had the same waiter. I was beginning to get that de ja' vu feeling, a feeling that doesn't sit too well on an empty stomach. What were the odds, I thought to myself, of lightning striking the same person, at the same "Popular eating joint," in the same room, with the same waiter...twice in a row? It had to be a trillion to 1. That kind of stuff just doesn't happen.

Presently, Eugene returned to our table bringing with him our overpriced breakfast. As he slid the plates of food into their respective places, I noticed how barren the table now looked in comparison to the way it used to be. Eugene must have read my mind for he commented, "It doesn't look like it did before, does it?" There was almost a gleam in his eye as he said it.

"No," I retorted, "what happened, wasn't corporate making enough money?" Thankfully, he let it drop and swished away from our table. Left alone, for the moment, we began performing, "The Ritual of the Grits."

There was just the right amount of sweetener to be mixed in them, exactly three packets of splenda, and then exactly one tub of butter. It was also important that these things be thoroughly stirred into the grits and that the butter be allowed to melt and mix all down in there before eating. After the Ritual of the Grits, we settled in to a nice breakfast. With chit-chat and small talk flying back and forth across the table. We ate our breakfast as we enjoyed each other's company and the morning sunlight coming in through the windows beside us. I had finished about half of my grits when I caught sight of something odd down deeper in the bowl. There was something in there that just wasn't the right color. The apprehension immediately began to grow in my mind as I recalled my last experience here with a bowl of grits. Could it be possible? It was really just too far-fetched to be believable. Digging down deeper into the bowl with my spoon, I retrieved one of those little, cigar shaped black things, and it wasn't a burnt grain of rice......Lightning, had struck twice in the same place. I had to be absolutely sure, though. So I dug it out, and put the little cigar on my napkin. Next, I took my knife and kind of smeared it a little bit. I was right the first time, it was yet another mouse turd. I was flabbergasted. What actually were the chances?

Donna immediately began getting Eugene's attention.

"Don't do that," I said, "there's no way in the world that he's gonna believe that I didn't put that in there, it just don't happen twice in a row."

I was too late, though, she had already caught his eye and he was on his way over.

"What can I do for you?" Eugene said, arriving at our table.

"Well, partner, do you remember, about a year and a half ago, you were waiting tables in this very room and a couple was sitting at that table right over there," I said pointing at the table in question, "and the guy pulled a mouse turd out of his grits?"

"Yes," he said, "I remember."

"Well," I said, "I was that guy, and today is my first time back since then....and I just found another mouse turd in my grits."

"No way," he said, without the slightest bit of emotion on his face.

"Yeah, way," I said, and holding up the napkin I said, "take a look for yourself."

It was plain that he didn't believe me, if I had been in his shoes, I probably wouldn't have believed it either. He just joked about how clean his kitchen was and how a mouse turd might have come in through their supplier, but certainly not because there might be a mouse in the building. I didn't think it strange, at the time, and given the circumstances, but he never once addressed the fact that there was a mouse turd in one of his customer's food. He seemed to be saying, "Shit happens."

I was done. I wasn't nearly so upset about the turd in my food as I was the fact that I had voluntarily returned to the same place where it had happened to me once before, and next, was the nonchalant manner in which "Management" treated the situation.

Leaving a customary tip, Donna and I left the table and went to the front to pay our bill. As always, the lady behind the cash register asked, "Was everything alright?"

"Everything was fine," I said, "right up till the time I found the mouse shit in my grits, for the second time in as many visits."

"Oh, my God," she exclaimed, "that's terrible."

"Not nearly as terrible for you as it is for me." I said.

"Let me get the manager," she said.

"Look," I said, "don't bother." What's she gonna do, offer to give me a discount? She didn't the last time this happened. The waiter acted as though he couldn't care less, so I just have to assume that this place doesn't care if the customer finds shit in their food. "I paid for it the last time, and I'm not trying to get something for nothing. I certainly intend to pay for my meal this time."

By this time the manager had shown up and I had to tell the whole story again. Just as I had predicted, it was just terrible, it was just awful, but it wasn't terrible or awful enough to offer to try to make things right. I guess that they like me thought that the chances of that happening twice in a row was so small that the only other plausible explanation was that I had put it in my own meal in order to get it free...which wasn't true! Of course! But if I had been in their shoes, I probably would have thought the same thing. It was just too far out of the ordinary to be believed.

My parting words to the manager were, "I, will not be back. You, have lost a customer, permanently. Not because of any issue in your kitchen, things are brought in shipping, and you have no control over that, but because of your total lack of interest when a customer comes to you with a complaint of this nature. Mouse shit in my food? You have got to be kidding me!"

I was 73 years old.......

Haircut

The dawn on Thursday morning, December 9th, 2021, was a grey affair. The clouds, pushing in from the Northwest, promised nothing but gloom and maybe some rain. It was characteristically cold outside, and I looked at it. The grass, that was now a brown color, had a thin skin of frost and no sun promised to melt it off. It was one of those days that was tailor made for sleeping, or at the very least pulling the thick covers up tighter around your neck for just a few minutes more. It was in this setting that I lay, enjoying the warmth of those covers as I contemplated, the "Cousins Luncheon" that Donna and I were to attend tomorrow.

The "Cousins Luncheon" was just an informal gathering of anyone who was a descendent of David and Josephine (Spivey) Suits or David and Rosa (Sims) Suits, and no invitation was necessary. We had been to one of these luncheons the previous year and had enjoyed it very much. It had been held at The Red Onion, a restaurant in the little town of Equality Illinois. It was at this gathering that I met Fred Suits, the son of my father's cousin, Charlie Suits. This year, we were going to be meeting more folks that we never knew existed.

As I lay there, all snug in my covers, Donna, who had been up for at least an hour, comes into my little comfortable piece of heaven with a rush and says, "You've got to get up and wash your hair. You need a haircut."

"What makes you think that I need a haircut?" I said, displeased that she wanted me to get out from under those warm covers. "There's nothing wrong with my hair."

"You can't go down there tomorrow looking like you do. Your hair is hanging over your ears and your collar. C'mon, get up, let's get it over with."

Realizing that she was probably right, and grumbling with every move, I reluctantly obeyed.

Only a month or so ago I had bought (At her request) a brand, spanking, new set of hair clippers, the kind that comes with all of those different, clip-on, plastic doo-dads –what lets you take off just a little tiny bit at a time, all the way down to a whole bunch at a time. These clippers came highly recommended by our local Aldi grocery store and sold for the unbelievably low price of just $20.00. Donna had taken one look at those things and she says, "I have got to have me some of them."

Now, I love my wife and I want to see her happy, so when we got home with the groceries, it was no surprise when out of one of those shopping bags came a set of those clippers. When she first got those things, she was anxious to try them out so she cut my hair...she did a pretty good job too. It was her first time an' she was careful, tryin' to do good. She didn't take off too much, just enough to make it look like I'd had a nice trim, she did good.

This morning, I had no reason to believe that she would do anything any different than the first time. So, I obediently oiled up her new clippers, sat down in that chair an' waited for her to decide which one of them plastic doo-dads she was gonna clip over the business edge of them clippers and go to whackin' on my freshly washed hair. She decided on ol" #7, the one what takes off the least amount of hair. She was happily buzzing through my silver locks and little wads of white were soon cascading down over the high quality, narrow plastic bib that came with these highly recommended, unbelievably low-priced clippers. We began to talk as she clipped and changed to another little plastic doo-dad.

"Now, don't cut it too short." I'd say, an' she'd answer, "Just let me cut it, I'm not stupid." Sufficiently chastened, I sat still and let her continue.

It wasn't until she put the little slanted doo-dad on the clippers that I got just a little apprehensive. I could see from the way they were slanted that maybe she should be going around my ears from the back to the front, instead of from the front to the back, (a small detail in the minds of some, but, trust me, and this comes from a veteran of many, many, haircuts), it makes all the difference in the world.

She next decided that in order to fix what had just happened; she needs to put on one of them shorter doo-dads and just free hand it. Well sir, there was nothing I could do but let her continue and hope that it would be alright.... I was wrong again. As a new set of little white wads began to cascade down that high quality plastic bib, I began to worry, just a little, about whether or not I would have enough hair left to comb.

I heard the tell-tale click of another doo-dad. Almost in a panic now, I began to squirm around in my seat like frog legs in a skillet of hot grease.

"Are you about through?" I asked.

"Almost!" she said as she clipped on another doo-dad. Each "Click" meant that my hair was getting progressively shorter. I had to do something, but what?

Finally, and thankfully, she said, "There." I lunged out of that chair, the high-quality plastic bib looking like a flag tied around my neck and waving in the breeze. I grabbed the closest mirror and I remember my very first thought being, "When did we get a molting Cockatoo?" I was gazing into the face of someone who was vaguely familiar, but this guy had the mange. It was at this point that the idea that I could fix it by myself came into my mind, another in the long string of bad decisions.

Snatching up those highly recommended, unbelievably low-priced clippers and a few select doo-dads, I headed for the bedroom where I had a big medicine cabinet with three mirrored doors. Anyone who is familiar with these things knows that the two outside doors open to where you can see both sides of your head, in reverse, key words there, "In Reverse." Plugging those clippers into the wall receptacle and hitting the "on" switch, I frantically tried to make the cockatoo turn into a recognizable person. Realizing at once that my wife's ability to cut my hair was far, far greater than my own, I finally regained control of my faculties and allowed her to kinda "Shorten it all over" to get rid of all my mistakes.

Finally finished, and knowing that it would eventually grow out, I accepted the fact that I would look a little different at the cousin's luncheon. Evidently, it wasn't as bad as all that because no one seemed to notice that the hair on the little, short fat guy was all but gone. On the other hand, it just might have been that everyone there was showing incredible courtesy by not whispering behind their hands or outright laughing at the hairless wonder who had dared to show up at the luncheon. Next time, we would both be more careful.

I was seventy three years old.......

I Was Here

When Eldorado has an Ice-House
When Eldorado had a Dr. Pepper Bottling Company
When lawn mowers had no motors
When shoes were re-soled, not thrown away
When shoe heels had metal plates put on them to keep the heel from wearing out
When Kerosene was used as a medicine
When every school day began with the Pledge of Allegiance
When Converse All Stars were the best tennis shoes to be found
Before people were sue-crazy
Before transistor radios
Before the first heart transplant
When people sat up with the dead.... (Called, A Wake)
When the first Super-Bowl was played
When personal Honor was a big deal
When "Macho" wasn't the "In-Thing," it was the "Only Thing"
When coal heated many, many homes
When a cook stove fueled by wood was common
When Eldorado jail was in use
When Mt. St. Helens erupted
In the same year that Israel reclaimed her status as a nation
When the Korean War broke out
When abortion was a back-alley procedure that wasn't talked about openly
When the population of the earth was a third of what it is today
When families gathered at Grandma and Grandpa's house on the weekends
Before Polaroid Camera
When almost everyone dried their clothes on a clothes line
When women used clothes pin bags

When most people used a wringer type washer
When lots of people made their own ice cream
When feather beds and hand-made quilts were common bed covers
When the original weed eaters were called Weed Hooks
Before Bloods and Crips, or motorcycle gangs
Before ice makers in refrigerators
When everybody used ice trays in their freezers
When Halloween candy was safe from razor blades and needles
When 8 inch snowfalls were very common in Southern Illinois
Before White Male was the most discriminated against.... (Opinion)
When life was lived at a much slower pace, it was much, much more laid back
Before microwave ovens
When all commercial airplanes had propellers
When railroads were a major source of transportation in America
When the south was still segregated
When all country roads in Saline County were gravel
When Eldorado Reservoir was a "Hot" fishing spot
When growing a garden was a necessity for lots of folks.
When kids had shoes that were for school only
When kids were to be seen and not heard
Before Elvis Presley had a singing career
When Rock-n-Roll was actually Rock-n-Roll
When Doo-Wop first came out
When Country Music was actually Country Music
When nylon hose had a seam up the back
When nurses wore a white dress and hat
When home perms were a big thing
When women used wave clamps in their hair
When Cat-Eye glasses frames were the latest in women's eye wear
When Dodge made the last DeSoto
When Corvette, Thunderbird, and Mustang first came out
Before cars had padded dashes
Before radial tires
Before Disc Brakes
When Ford made The Edsel

When Ford made the Hard-Top Convertible
When all cars and truck had wing glasses
When cars were made of American steel
When cars were much bigger
When Highways were much smaller
When hitting a deer with a car, didn't total the car
When no car had a plastic bumper
When Hudson "Hornet" was still being made
Before Interstate Highways
When the speed limit on two-lane highways was 65 MPH
When the small farmer could make living from his land
When many country folks would preserve their own meat
When some folks took what they called "Shower Baths" under a garden hose
When taking a bath in a wash tub was common
When outdoor toilets were common, even in town
When some people had outside toilets with two seats, they were called Two Holers
When making Sorghum-Molasses was a common practice
Before big round bales of hay
When hauling hay paid a half cent a bale
When almost every farm had a corn crib
When wearing a cowboy hat didn't make a guy a Cowboy
When there were still Rustlers out west
Before all these gun laws
Before the FOID card was even an idea
When anyone could buy ammo and shot-shells from any old country store
When kids 8 or 10 years old could, and did, hunt with their dads and uncles
When every honeysuckle covered fence-row was full of rabbits or birds
When laziness was the exception, not the rule
When Kareem Abdul Jabbar's name was Lew Alcindor
When Muhammed Ali's name was Cassius Clay
When the students at Kent State University were shot, and killed, by the National Guard
When Pat O'Connor was killed at the Indianapolis 500
When the first satellite (Sputnik) went into space
When there were only 48 states

When school teachers used the paddle, liberally
Before personal computers
Before cell-phones were even an idea
When Sabre Jets were downing Russian Migs in Mig Alley, Korea
When Rocky Marciano was the Heavyweight Champ
When Iran was the friend of America
When the Berlin Wall was built
When the Berlin Wall was taken down
Before AIDS
When Harry Truman was President
When Brylcreem, Wildroot Cream Oil, Butch Wax, or Vitalis was a must for boys
When the hip pocket of every teenaged boy contained a comb
Before plastic sandwich bags
Before Television was common in American homes
Before Air-Conditioning was common in American homes
Before police cars had blue lights
Before the Korean War
Before man first walked on the moon
Before the "All Volunteer Army"
Before the "Bay of Pigs Invasion"
Before the Cuban Missile Crisis
When John F. Kennedy was assassinated
Before automatic transmissions were common in cars
Before power steering was available in cars
When the one-roomed school was still very common
Before mandatory bussing
Before the Viet-Nam war
Before the DA hair doo was the style
When a closet was for hanging clothes in, not for coming out of
When Coke was a soda pop, not a white powder
When there were no drive by shootings
When drugs were a minor problem at the worst
When Polio was very dangerous, and, very common
When people went to Sanitariums when they had Tuberculosis
When everyone picked up Hitch-Hikers

When a man with long hair was considered feminine
When only the female gender wore ear-rings
Before the Feminist Movement
When people sat around the radio for entertainment
When there really were Door to Door Salesmen
Before Girls High School Sports
When America's coins were made of silver, not a mixture
When smoking was allowed everywhere, except in church
When Homosexuality was a shame, not an alternative lifestyle

Where Love Goes

Where is that place, where young love goes,
When youth had fled away?
That place where kisses lingered,
Sweet as honey, every day?
Where did it go, that time of ours,
When every day was bliss?
When every hurtful word was washed, Away, with just a kiss?
Where is that place, where you and I
Held hands beneath the stars?
That place we thought we'd always be,
That place that we called ours?
Where is that place, of plans and dreams,
Where hopes and wishes grew?
Where has it gone, this wonderland
Where love was always new?
"Alas, it's gone, it's gone," you cry,
"It's gone forevermore,"
But wait, sweetheart, and listen,
It's not gone, it's only stored.

There is a place, where these things go
A place where they're kept safe.
Your youth is there, your silken touch,
Your voice, your lovely face.
This place contains the good things,
Untarnished, untouched by time.
It keeps a picture of the day,

When first, your heart was mine.
"Where is this place?" you ask me.
"Can I go? Is it far?"
Why, sweetheart, you can go right now,
You see, it's in my heart
There's only one way to this place,
And you have to only key,
And I only ask one thing of you....
When you go....Please, take me....
John M Suits 3/3/2008

My Love

Come, talk to me, let me hear the sweetness of your voice again, before my world grows silent, forever.....

Come, touch me, let the smoothness of your hand linger on my face and restore my youth, if only for an instant.....

Come, caress me, let your silver locks brush against my chest and make me tremble, as in days gone by.....

Come, look at me, let me see, once again the twinkle in your eye that was my treasure so long ago.....

Come, smile at me, let me once more drink at the fountain of your beauty, as I did when we were young.....

It is enough

The Trip

He lies awake at night, remembering, every second under fire,
the "silent sounds" the Sappers made, when comin' through the wire,
the peculiar "Snap" a bullet makes, when passing overhead,
the putrid stench of burning flesh, when countin' up the dead.
"Get some sleep" they told him, "for they'll hit us at first light,"
He never got to close his eyes, they came all through the night,
And when the rays of morning sun,
lit up that ghastly field,
He marveled, midst the horror, that he too wasn't killed.
He lives in two worlds, always, and his family doesn't
know, that he makes a journey, nightly, to that field of long ago.
Where he walks and talks with brothers, takes The Point, every now and
then.....
runs for cover, where there is none from the mortars comin' in.
He can hear the noise of battle,
see the green of traces rounds,
he can see his brothers falling,
twisted, bleeding...to the ground.
Charlie grabs him by the shoulder, he quickly rises from the deck,
And his wife's face comes in focus, just before he snaps her neck.
He apologizes, quickly, sheds a tear for all those friends.....
And dreads the coming of tomorrow.....
When he'll make "The Trip" again
John M Suits 10/20/2001

Home Growed Vittles

So, my wife goes out to the garden an' grabs up a couple o' them big ol' high pink Mortgage Lifter tomaters, an' a few o' them there long, sweet banana peppers. When she comes in the house she says to me, she says, "Git yo hide on up out o thet there chair an' hep me put on vittles." Well sir, I mosey on into the kitchen, an' after a runnin' my hands through some soapy water, I takes a look around an' I sees, right away thet she's already got stuff washed up an' ready fer my knife, so I jest lites into carvin' on some o' them there taters.

I cuts some o' them there taters real thin, so's a body can read a paper through 'em. (I like some of 'em real crunchy like.) Some o' the others I cuts up kinda thick an' slabby, the way my wife likes 'em. Next, I takes a big ol' onion an' one o' them there long sweet banana peppers an' I cuts 'em up an' I flung 'em down in thet skillet with all them taters. We had us a couple o' slabs o' them there hog steaks a cookin' out on the grill with some more o' them there peppers. Donna, thet's my wife's name, Donna, well she done carved up them tomaters an' took the peelin' off 'n them squashes what we had a settin on the table, an' she done mixed up some aig an' milk so's I could swab them big ol' thick slices o' squash down in it afore I flung 'em into the corn meal. Well sir, I looks, an' bless yo life, I ain't got nary bit o' lard, so I takes an' uses some o' thet oil what comes in one o' them new fangled plastic jugs, an' I heats it up real good so's it'll put a good scald on my squashes, an' I drops 'em in. Lawdy, my kitchen is a smellin' good right about now. In just a little while, we sets down to fried taters, fried squashes, home growed tomaters, peppers an' them there hog steaks.....my, my, my.....after jest a little bit, them taters, squashes, tomaters an' peppers was gone without a trace....an' them hog steaks, well, they jest got wrapped up fer another day. They jest ain't hardly nothin' better to wrap yo tongue around, than home growed vittles.......I makes me a note in that little note book what I keeps in my bibs..... "Be sure to git me some lard at the next hog killin'."

John M. Suits 2015

Rocks

Ok, so my little four year old Great Granddaughter is out "Helping" her Pappaw in the garden. She picks up a "Big People's Hoe" and laboriously tears up the dirt and drags it into a pile. When she has built a mound of what she considers sufficient size, she stops, finds a piece of brown river gravel, looks up at me and says, "Pappaw, I'm gonna bury this rock."

Now, I, thinking to get a good giggle out of her answer, asked, "Do you think it's gonna grow Honey?" She stops in the middle of her ceremony, looks up at me with those big, blue eyes, gives me that all knowing smile that only a four year old is capable of, and as sweetly as the cherub that I think she is, says to me, "Rocks don't grow, silly." She must be right, I must be "silly" because days later, I still haven't gotten that good giggle that I was thinking about, and instead, I'm still wondering why in the world did she bury that rock?

The best reason that I can come up with is....She's four years old....it ain't rocket science.....they do stuff like that. Outdone by a four year old, I must be getting old. I'll accept that, though, because.....it's HER.

John M. Suits 4/17/2014